THE MILITARY
AND THE MEDIA

THE MILITARY
and the MEDIA

Why the Press Cannot Be Trusted to Cover a War

WILLIAM V. KENNEDY

Westport, Connecticut
London

P
96
.A752
U65
1993

Library of Congress Cataloging-in-Publication Data

Kennedy, William V.
    The military and the media : why the press cannot be trusted to
cover a war / William V. Kennedy.
        p.   cm.
    Includes bibliographical references and index.
    ISBN 0–275–94191–4 (alk. paper)
    1. Armed Forces and mass media—United States.   2. War in the
press—United States.   I. Title.
P96.A752U65   1993
070.4′49355—dc20   92–46555

British Library Cataloguing in Publication Data is available.

Library of Congress Catalog Card Number: 92–46555
ISBN: 0–275–94191–4

First published in 1993

Praeger Publishers, 88 Post Road West, Westport, CT 06881
An imprint of Greenwood Publishing Group, Inc.

Printed in the United States of America

The paper used in this book complies with the
Permanent Paper Standard issued by the National
Information Standards Organization (Z39.48–1984).

10 9 8 7 6 5 4 3 2 1

In Memoriam
Jerimiah L. O'Sullivan
Dean of the College of Journalism
Marquette University
1928–1962

The function of journalism is not to tell
the drowning man that the dam has broken, or to warn the community that the
dam is cracked and that they should run
for the hills. The function of journalism is
to warn the community that the dam is in
danger of cracking.

—The O'Sullivan Rule

Contents

Introduction

Every time a society has permitted its military establishment to insulate itself against effective public scrutiny that military establishment has ended up destroying the people it was supposed to protect. As classical scholars steeped in the process by which the Roman republic became a military dictatorship, and as grandsons of a generation that saw a military dictatorship established in England under Oliver Cromwell, the American Founding Fathers sought to write into the U.S. Constitution a set of checks and balances that they hoped would immunize the new Republic against this military virus.

The independence guaranteed to the press under the First Amendment to that Constitution is one of the most important of those safeguards. Yet every bureaucrat knows that power flows from each increment of information he or she can garner and hold tight. To the extent that our society permits such bureaucratic self-interest to restrict access by the public to the business of government—in particular its military business—the First Amendment becomes meaningless.

Very few citizens have the time and means to search out government information vital to their well-being. As a result, access means mainly access by the press, like it or not.

During the months leading up to the Persian Gulf War of 1990–91 and throughout the war itself the U.S. government succeeded, for the first time in U.S. history, in controlling almost totally what the public would be permitted to know about the conduct of military operations. That happened not because government is as yet all-powerful, but because a smug, arrogant, and self-righteous press was operating twentieth- and twenty-first-century technology with nineteenth-century concepts of organization, training, and management.

In a speech to the National Newspaper Association following the end of the war, General Colin L. Powell, chairman of the U.S. Joint Chiefs of Staff, acknowledged that if the Iraqi army had moved, in August 1990, as it was entirely capable of doing, to occupy the principal Saudi Arabian airfields and ports, the United States would have been in enormous difficulty. What General Powell did not tell his audience, but what Major General Edward B. Atkeson, formerly of the Central Intelligence Agency, had made plain more than three years earlier in an article in *Armed Forces Journal International*[1] was that for a period of several weeks, until major U.S. land and air forces could be inserted, a determined, large-scale Iraqi invasion could be stopped only by nuclear weapons.

But American journalism has neither the technical competence to recognize the long-term implications of an article such as General Atkeson's nor the structural means to relate it to a crisis that occurs years, or even months, later. So the public—American or otherwise—was never informed that in declaring his intention to defeat Iraqi aggression the president of the United States was, in fact, committing the United States to nuclear war during the period when the first token U.S. land forces flown to the region were in danger of being overrun.

As with every major military story since the end of World War II, the press failed. It did not fail because of government censorship. Rather, it failed because of the inadequacies of its own training and organization, deficiencies that prevented it from reporting matters of crucial importance, even when all of the essential facts were in the public domain.

It was also during the Persian Gulf War that the government demonstrated the means to black out the battlefield any time it so chooses, even in the presence of hundreds of representatives of the world press. When a television reporter watching the takeoff of U.S. fighters from a Saudi base began to report that one of the fighters appeared to be experiencing mechanical trouble, his satellite link was shut down by military electronic countermeasures.

Deriving partly from its enormous resources, but mainly from its dereliction of the press itself, the U.S. military is now in a position to dictate how its wars are reported. As in Ceasar's time, therein lies the path to political power. Indeed, General Powell and the operational commander, General H. Norman Schwarzkopf, were being touted for high political office before the war was fairly over.

Those most visible of the generals who led the U.S. and allied coalition to victory in the Persian Gulf War would seem unlikely candidates for the sort of absolute power Julius Ceasar would attain. There is a curious irony in that: The three military principals of the Persian Gulf War—Generals Powell and Schwarzkopf and Lieutenant General Thomas W. Kelly, the operations chief of the Joint Staff and its principal public spokesman—reached high rank precisely because they possess the personalities required to function effectively in an open, democratic society. It was no accident that they were all from the Army. Whether it draws its soldiers from a draft or a volunteer system, the Army must be more closely attuned to the society it serves than must the more technically oriented Navy and Air Force.

To the degree that it succeeds in insulating itself from close public scrutiny the Army will become more like its more uptight sister services and will move steadily closer to the Prussian model that brought Germany to disaster in two world wars. It will be an Army in which a Powell, a Schwarzkopf, or a Kelly would be unlikely to rise above lieutenant colonel.

At least since the early 1960s the press has been unable to assess accurately the mass of military data that was already on the public record. Given that dismal record it is difficult to see how the U.S. military leadership at the time of the Gulf War could have failed to take drastic action to limit press coverage when mistakes of assessment could have tragic consequences.

It was said ruefully, and truly, by Ron Nessen, vice president for news at NBC Radio/Mutual Broadcasting, when the degree of press exclusion became clear that "The Pentagon has won the last battle of the Vietnam War. It was fought in the sands of Saudi Arabia, and the defeated enemy was us."[2] How totally the military has gained control is described in Chapter 1.

Vietnam is indeed the watershed between the relatively open access by the press during all previous U.S. wars and the tightly controlled access imposed during the Persian Gulf War. Understanding how that happened is absolutely crucial to understanding what must be done to restructure the press so that it can regain the confidence of the American public, for it was the loss of such confidence that enabled the military to impose the controls that it did during the Gulf War.

The deep structural defects that led to the disastrous Vietnam press coverage existed long before U.S. forces became engaged in Southeast Asia and were apparent in every major military news story up to that time. These are discussed in Chapters 2 through 6. What went wrong in Vietnam is discussed in Chapter 7, and how that led to exclusion or total government management of the press in Grenada, Panama, and the Persian Gulf is described in Chapter 8.

The establishment of a "right to lie" as official U.S. government policy during the administration of President John F. Kennedy and the elaborate systems available to pursue such a policy, made all the more dangerous by the absence of effective press surveillance, are discussed in Chapter 9. The final chapter describes what could be done if an aroused citizenry were to force the owners of the nation's major news media to address the problem.

NOTES

1. Edward B. Atkeson, "The Persian Gulf: Still a Vital U.S. Interest?" *Armed Forces Journal International* 114 (April 1987): 46–56. See also Benjamin J. Schem-

mer, "Was the U.S. Ready to Resort to Nuclear Weapons for the Persian Gulf in 1980?" *Armed Forces Journal International* 113 (September 1986): 92–105.

2. Ron Nessen, "The Pentagon Censors" (Op-Ed), *Washington Post*, 12 January 1991.

THE MILITARY
AND THE MEDIA

1

Why the Press Cannot Be Trusted to Cover a War

During a period of seventy-two hours, February 25–27, 1991, a revolution occurred in the waging of war. That revolution, which had immediate and profound implications for every American in terms of the cost and effectiveness of national defense, occurred in the full view of over 1,000 representatives of the U.S. and international press; yet not one reported its significance. And, because of that, status-quo forces within the U.S. Army were able to gain continued funding for billions of dollars worth of programs that were now patently obsolete.

It was not as though the revolution had burst out so suddenly that it was impossible to immediately assess its dimensions or its significance. As early as 1960, Army public affairs officers in the Pentagon were directing any journalist who seemed interested to the namesake of a distinguished Confederate general, Albert Sidney Johnson.[1] This new Albert Syndey Johnson was a lieutenant colonel assigned to the Air Mobility Branch of what was then the Office of the Deputy Chief of Staff for Force Development. He talked in terms of a vision: "A war fought one foot above the ground" in self-contained aerial equivalents of the tank and the armored personnel carrier.

Only six years after the U.S. Army had become imprisoned once again in World War I–style trench warfare in the latter stages of the Korean War, Johnson was talking about "getting the Army out of the mud," a goal to be achieved by development of an aerial vehicle—the helicopter—that was then about as far along as the tank had been in the 1920s.

Those who did not dismiss the vision out of hand were directed to Brigadier General Sam Shaw, then chief of landing force development for the U.S. Marine Corps. General Shaw was more than happy to describe how the Marine Corps was using the helicopter to develop a concept of "vertical envelopment," landing Marines behind the enemy beach defenses that had taken such a toll at Tarawa and Normandy in World War II. And General Shaw was happy to take anyone who showed a continuing interest to Fort Rucker, Alabama, where the Army was taking the helicopter one step further by strapping machine guns and rocket pods to its fuselage—closing the loop that had started at Lieutenant Colonel Johnson's desk.

It was a journalistically lonely path. With but one exception, no member of the national news media had taken an interest in the story. The exception was Lynn Montross, a writer whose interest was primarily in military affairs and who had seen the possibilities even before the Army public affairs officers began trying to awaken such interest. Montross's small book, *Cavalry of the Sky*, had been noted by Hanson W. Baldwin, then nominally the military "editor" of the *New York Times*. But that glimmer of interest had died when Baldwin went into retirement after fighting a hopeless rearguard battle within the *Times* staff for honest, professional military reporting.

To anyone who had taken the time to listen to such visionaries as Johnson and Shaw, the development of the military helicopter during the succeeding decades took on an entirely different meaning than was the case with those who seemed to think that the military was simply finding new uses for the helicopter as new technology appeared. And to those few journalists who had read carefully such publications as *Army* magazine, the privately published weekly newspaper *Army Times*, and the armor and aviation branch journals of the army, something else became readily apparent: The senior U.S. Army leadership was determined that its nascent helicopter aviation arm would not develop as had the old Army Air Corps, which had broken away in 1947 to form a separate, competing U.S. Air Force.

The new generation of Army aviators, flying helicopters and the few fixed-wing aircraft the Air Force had left behind, was to be kept in a "support" role, with personnel parceled out among the major land force branches—infantry, armor, and artillery—and thereby threatening none of the traditional, non-aviation career patterns. It was repetition of the manner in which tanks had been parceled out, in the 1920s and 1930s, so as not to upset the traditional bureaucratic establishments of the day, then primarily the infantry and the horse cavalry. In the present context, there would be no "war fought one foot above the ground" if the tankers, the walking infantry, and, above all, the parachutists—in reality the least mobile of all Army forces once they leave the airplane—could help it.

The parachute (airborne) infantry had become the post–World War II Army's school of daring, a role performed prior to World War II by the polo-playing horse cavalry. Never mind that most division-level airborne operations in World War II were unmitigated disasters. And never since that war has there been a parachute infantry operation larger than a two-battalion brigade, always against lightly defended targets.

But, like the horse cavalry of the 1930s, the airborne became the emotional focus of those who wanted to believe that courage and daring would always prevail over technology. So thoroughly dominated has the post–World War II Army been by the parachute mentality that, to this day, a hugely expensive parachute infantry establishment is maintained in the hope that somewhere, somehow it might prove useful. Nothing so mesmerizes the press as a mass parachute jump. It has tagged along with the airborne myth like a faithful puppy.

Despite all that, Army aviators managed to obtain authorization for a study under the leadership of General Hamilton Howze that would prove to be the cornerstone of spectacular performance during the Gulf War by a new air cavalry. American journalism outside of the military publications was oblivious to all this. But others were not.

In June 1983 General Ferdinand M. von Senger und Etterlin, then commanding the NATO Central Army Group, proposed restructuring NATO land forces on the model of the U.S. Sixth Air Cavalry Brigade.[2] The latter is a force proposed by General Howze and designed around derivatives of the attack helicopters with which the Army had been experimenting since the 1950s. Armed with machine guns, rockets, and a long-range anti-tank guided missile (the Hellfire), the most modern of these aircraft—notably the U.S. AH–64 Apache—can now outmaneuver and outfight any of the world's tanks. Combined with scout and troop-carrying helicopters, this new air cavalry can deliver heliborne infantry, engineers, and artillery deep into enemy territory, blocking the escape routes of enemy forward units and cutting their logistical lifelines.

As a young officer, General von Senger und Etterlin had seen the German panzers isolate and immobilize superior, but hopelessly immobile, Allied forces in northern France in June 1940. He saw in the attack helicopter the same 20–1 advantage in mobility and firepower that had proven decisive for the World War II tank and armored infantry units.

Having come to essentially the same conclusion, British Brigadier Richard E. Simpkin went one step further and proposed in 1985 that the United States deploy air cavalry brigades aboard large aircraft carriers.[3] On August 13, 1990, eleven days after Iraq invaded Kuwait, France upstaged its U.S. ally by doing exactly that.

While the United States was still cramming its attack helicopters into large transport aircraft, requiring substantial disassembly and subsequent reassembly, France flew its Fifth Attack Helicopter Regiment onto the deck of the large aircraft carrier *Clemenceau*.[4] Had the regiment not been held at Djibouti in Northeastern Africa so that the French government could make up its mind how deeply it wanted to become involved, the Fifth Regiment with the *Clemenceau* as a continuing base for maintenance, ammunition supply, and medical and other logistical support would have been in position, ready to fight, weeks before the United States managed to assemble a comparable capability.

At least two U.S. carriers were available for similar service. They were not used, first, because the U.S. Army had nowhere near the faith in its attack helicopter arm that von Senger und Etterlin, Simpkin, and now the French had expressed and, second, because the basing of an Army combat aviation unit aboard a large carrier is anathema to the U.S. Navy and Marine Corps. They would see it as an infringement on the most fundamental of all Navy–Marine Corps doctrines: that the sea services constitute a single, inviolable whole sufficient in all respects unto themselves and warranting no "intrusions" by the Army or anyone else.

The departure of the Fifth Attack Helicopter Regiment aboard the *Clemenceau* was fully reported. Yet no member of the U.S. press in either Saudi Arabia or Washington grasped the significance of the event, even though the issues had been spelled out during the early days of the Persian Gulf deployments in *Christian Science Monitor*[5] and *Newsday*[6] opinion page commentaries that were transmitted nationwide by the Washington Post–Los Angeles Times New Service.

Even in the dire emergency that prevailed in Saudi Arabia during August and into September 1990, the U.S. Army was determined not to give the attack helicopter the central role that von Senger und Etterlin, Simpkin, and many of its own senior aviators were demanding. Except for the misnamed 101st Airborne Division, now wholly built around attack, scout, troop-carrying, and transport helicopters, there would be no massing of attack helicopters under a single aviation command. All other attack helicopter units would be firmly subordinated to conventional mechanized infantry, armored, and airborne commands, reinforcing the status quo and the careers invested therein.

For at least two weeks after the Iraqi invasion of Kuwait on August 2 nothing but a slim, inexperienced, and inadequately organized Saudi Arabian force stood between the Iraqi armored formations and the airfields and ports required to receive the promised allied reinforcements. Advance elements of the U.S. 82d Airborne Division had begun to arrive on August 8, but neither then nor at any time during the remainder of the war would the paratroopers—essentially lightly armed, dismounted infantry—have been able to do more than delay for a matter of a few hours, at most, any determined armored attack on the ports and airfields they were assigned to guard.

For several years U.S. Marine Corps equipment had been "prepositioned" aboard ships permanently anchored at the island grouping of Diego Garcia in the Indian Ocean. Marines were airlifted to Saudi Arabia and the ships gotten underway from Diego Garcia at the same time the 82d Airborne Division advance elements began to arrive. But, like the 82d, the Marines, once ashore, are essentially dismounted infantry. Although the first Marines arrived on August 14, it was September 14 before their tanks and other heavy equipment arrived from Diego Garcia and were unloaded, distributed to units, and prepared for active service. Even then, the Marines, by the nature of their system of organization and doctrine, were incapable of moving more than a few miles inland and of establishing the broad, mobile "covering force" that would be necessary to block an armored blitzkrieg if that had materialized.

Thus, it was not until August 31, when a reinforced brigade of the U.S. 101st Airborne Division (Air Assault)[7] with 117 attack and transport helicopters was deemed ready to fight, that an adequate covering force began to materialize. To get that force with its supporting ground vehicles to Saudi Arabia had required sixty C–141 and fifty C–5A heavy air transport sorties. Had a U.S. aircraft carrier configured to transport that same force been stationed in an East Coast U.S. port, the time could have been halved, and a far more combat-capable force could have been delivered intact with far more ammunition, spare parts, and other logistical support immediately on hand than would be available in Saudi Arabia for weeks yet to come.

Indeed, it was not until October 15 that deployment of the entire 101st Division with all of its 116 attack helicopters was complete and the Division in a covering-force position. Only then did the U.S. command have some reasonable basis for believing that, together with the powerful air forces now in the theater of operations, it could defeat a mass armored attack.

Although nominally an infantry-heavy "Airborne" division, the principal combat power of the 101st lay in its attack and armed scout helicopters. But the misleading "Airborne" designation was enough to camouflage all that from the members of the press, many of whom would go on throughout the war reporting the 101st as "paratroopers."

Throughout August and at least most of September, only the instantaneous use of nuclear weapons at the Saudi-Kuwait border could have defeated a determined assault by the forces available to Iraq. Only the threat of nuclear force assured that the Iraqis would not destroy or imprison the tens of thousand of lightly armed Americans who had been deployed into the theater by air transport and who were mainly engaged in unloading other air and sea transport.

It required no access to classified information to determine well in advance the extent of that risk. It had been described in precise detail in a Congressional Budget Office (CBO) study published in 1983[8] and by a former highly placed Central Intelligence Agency analyst, Army Major General Edward B. Atkeson, in the April 1987 issue of *Armed Forces Journal International*. Although the significance of the Atkeson and CBO analyses had been discussed in detail on the opinion pages of the *Philadelphia Inquirer*,[9] *Newsday*,[10] and elsewhere, the "herd instinct" of mainstream American journalism is such that, without the imprimatur of page-one reporting by establishment writers in the *New York Times* or the *Washington Post*, no attempt is made to determine the validity of such warnings.

In all of the history of American journalism there has existed only one research center that would have been capable of retaining analyses such as the CBO report and the Atkeson article and of relating them months or years later to new events. As will be discussed in more detail in a later chapter, that center was deliberately destroyed during the internal struggle over defense reporting that occurred within the *New York Times* during the Vietnam War. Computers can amass and present huge quantities of information, but only trained human beings can arrive at implications. It was the loss of the human part of the equation during the internal struggle at the *Times* that cost American journalism what institutional memory it ever possessed concerning coverage of national defense.

Months into the Persian Gulf deployment, and with a vast sigh of relief, U.S. commanders began to admit the extreme degree of risk of those first few weeks in the Persian Gulf. Even then, the press did not inform the public of the fact that it had stood on the brink of nuclear war because the press itself lacked the training to grasp the implications of what the commanders were saying.

The most significant implication of all, of course, has been neither reported nor analyzed for the profound concerns it should incite for the future of democratic government: that the president of the United States, solely by the use of his powers as commander in Chief, had taken out of the hands of the public and the Congress and, eventually, even out of his own hands the most crucial of all modern decisions, resort to nuclear firepower. That is, from the moment those first few thousand vulnerable U.S. paratroopers and Marines arrived in Saudi Arabia the decision as to the use of nuclear firepower rested solely in the hands of the Iraqi leader, Saddam Hussein, whose troops could have made a dash for the Saudi ports and airfields before they were faced with an overwhelming allied counterforce on the ground. Any U.S. president who failed to use nuclear weapons, the only means available, to protect thousands of U.S. soldiers and Marines would have been impeached. That the Iraqi leader refrained from such action suggests that he fully understood the nuclear risks.

Thus, far from disappearing with the end of the Cold War, a significant threat of nuclear war exists across the entire span of possible future conflicts. That new dimension of the nuclear threat, with its requirement for continually modernized nuclear deterrent forces, would not receive the attention it deserved in the post–Gulf War U.S. defense debate because the press had failed to report the full dimensions of that threat during the early weeks of the Gulf War.

The U.S. and French air cavalry covering force in place by October 15 ultimately would prove to be the decisive combat force of the ground war. The U.S. commanders, however, continued to believe that heavy armored forces, slowly being assembled at enormous expense from the United States and Europe, were the "arm of decision" required to defeat the Iraqi army in Kuwait. In violation of all that had been learned from World War I onward about the need for centralized control of combat aviation, the Army and Marine commanders in the Gulf continued to deploy their attack helicopters in scattered increments, determined to keep them in their assigned "support" role.

Although some of its soldiers and a few armored vehicles had been flown to the Persian Gulf earlier, it was not until September that any significant part of the first large armored formation—the 24th Mechanized Division—was in place and ready to fight. It would take at least three additional months before the greater part of those forces could be deployed from the United States and Europe, reassembled, and retrained and before the enormous tonnages of ammunition and spare parts required to sustain them could be transported by sea.

It was the AH–64 Apache attack helicopter that began the war, and it was the Apache that ended it. Without early warning (EW) and ground-control-of-interception (GCI) radar a modern air force is blind and crippled, no matter how modern its aircraft and no matter how skilled and courageous its pilots. At 0230 hours on January 27, 1991, Apache attack helicopters of the 1st Battalion, 101st Aviation Battalion, 101st Airborne Division (Air Assault), under cover of U.S. Air Force fighter aircraft, struck the EW and GCI radars on which Iraq depended to provide air defense of its forces in Kuwait and the Iraqi homeland itself.[11] Fifteen of sixteen long-range Hellfire missiles fired by the Apaches found their mark. For all practical purposes, the Iraqi air force was dead.

Once the Iraqis were deprived of their own aerial reconnaissance and subject to continuous attack by allied aircraft, it was impossible for them either to learn what the allied commanders were doing or to reposition their own forces, even if they had been able to learn by some other means, such as spies, what the allies were doing. That set the stage for moving U.S. and French air cavalry forces far to the west, supposedly to "support" an attack by the 24th Mechanized Division into the Euphrates River valley, thereby trapping the Iraqi army in Kuwait.

In fact, when the allied ground attack began, it was the other way around. The U.S. and French attack helicopters devastated all Iraqi armored units in their path or, having cut them off from supply or retreat, left them to be destroyed or captured by "follow-on" armored, artillery, and infantry units. The pattern was exactly as General von Senger und Etterlin had foreseen it eight years before.

The 24th Mechanized Division never got closer than seven hours behind the attack helicopters and heliborne infantry and artillery of the 101st. Indeed, there is on tape an appeal form the commander of the lead brigade of the 24th Division to the commander of the attack helicopters to "leave something for us." Even more embarrassing, helicopter pilots noted that the advance vehicles of the 24th Division were not tanks and armored personnel carriers, but rather wheeled refueling trucks, racing ahead of the combat formations to assure refueling of the attack helicopters.

At 0600 hours on February 25, striking from a forward base occupied entirely by air assault, the Third Brigade of the 101st moved into the Euphrates River valley. In a matter of hours, heliborne infantry troops were athwart and had cratered Highway 8, one of the two main highways that were the lifeline of the Iraqi army in Kuwait. Because of a failure of coordination between U.S. Army and Air Force planners, however, an escape route had been left open to the Iraqi occupation forces in Kuwait City via a causeway leading north across Al Hammar Lake to at least the possibility of safety beyond the Euphrates.

"At about this time," according to an Army after-action report," [air reconnaissance] imagery revealed that the Iraqis had become aware that Highway 8 was blocked, and a series of huge Iraqi columns were detected turning and moving back to the north toward [the Al Hammar] four-lane causeway, now the only route left out of Kuwait. . . .

"The situation worsened when Air Force and Navy pilots reported that the Iraqis had fired the oil wells around the causeway and that visibility was dropping rapidly. Thousands of vehicles were clogged around the southern end of the causeway. . . .

"The nearest heavy Allied armored formation, the U.S. 24th Mechanized Infantry Division, was still three days away from the causeway. . . . "

With the U.S. Air Force and Navy fixed-wing fighter and attack aircraft blinded by the heavy smoke, the attack helicopter was the only feasible means of attacking the massed Iraqi columns. By another gigantic leap—this time of some 200 kilometers—logistics elements were jumped eastward from the original XVIII Airborne Corps area of operations into a new forward operating base (FOB Viper) to put attack helicopter battalions within range of the Al Hammar causeway.

Now occurred one of the profound ironies of the entire Desert Shield buildup and Persian Gulf War. For a variety of reasons, mainly involving problems of internal management, the Sixth Air Cavalry Brigade—the prototype unit on which General von Senger und Etterlin and Brigadier Simpkin had built their estimate of modern air cavalry potential—had not been deemed ready for deployment. Thus, until the emergence of the Al Hammar causeway crisis, most of the attack helicopters available to the allied command were still deployed piecemeal in the conventional "support" role. Threatened with the escape of a huge part of the Iraqi garrison in Kuwait, the XVIII Airborne Corps created what amounted to a provisional air cavalry brigade, massing six attack helicopter battalions drawn from their various "parent" divisions. Using external fuel tanks these were sent in relays 150 miles, round-trip, from the FOB Viper to block the Iraqi escape columns. It was those attacks that produced the horrific pictures of a causeway crammed with burned vehicles and blasted human remains that marked the destruction of the Iraqi army in Kuwait.

Most of the German army that overran Poland in 1939 and defeated the combined French, British, and Belgian armies in 1940 was still marching, or at best truck-borne infantry. Many of its artillery and logistics support vehicles were horse-drawn. The panzer (tank) divisions with their panzer-grenadiers (infantry riding in armored vehicles) were a relatively small part of that army, but, teamed with tactical air power and expertly employed under centralized control, they decided the issue of victory or defeat.

Allied heavy tanks, armored personnel carriers, and armored artillery were to the Persian Gulf War what the marching infantry and horse-drawn artillery had been to the German army of 1939–40. The allied armored units destroyed an enormous quantity of Iraqi war materiel in the Persian Gulf War and compelled the surrender of large numbers of prisoners. But the Iraqi army in Kuwait had already been doomed by the attack helicopter and the allied air forces.

Months after the war a controversy would emerge over the allies' failure to destroy the total Iraqi war machine. That debate focused on the withdrawal of many of the better Iraqi units—elements of the Republican Guard—to southern Iraq shortly after the Iraqis occupied Kuwait in August. When the allied forces were ordered by the U.S. high command in Washington to cease fire, the XVIII Airborne Corps was prepared, once again, to leapfrog American and French air cavalry north of Basra. Had this been permitted, the destruction of the Iraqi army would have been virtually complete.

All of the information pertaining to the spectacular success of the U.S. and French air cavalry was available to the entire press corps virtually as it happened. But neither then nor in the months after the war would any journalist raise what to the trained observer were the most obvious of questions:

1. Since the attack helicopter had demonstrated itself to be the decisive weapon both in the defense (covering force) operation and in the attack, why is the United States planning to spend billions to develop and produce another "family" of heavy armored vehicles?

2. Given the high level of strategic mobility demonstrated by French use of the *Clemenceau* and, to a less effective degree, by U.S. use of large, long-range air transports, why continue to maintain a large, heavily armored U.S. force in Germany with all that entails in terms of family support, schools, and recreational facilities? Can't the Europeans defend themselves at least for the few days needed to deploy U.S. air cavalry aboard aircraft carriers, via long-range air transport, or under their own power, or a combination of all three?

The U.S. Army aviators interviewed during and subsequent to the war were aching for those questions to be asked, but to no avail. Their comments evoked the memory of an Army public affairs colleague who, as he left a Pentagon news conference in the 1960s, sadly shook his head and commented, "They never ask the right questions." That comment would be repeated almost verbatim nearly thirty years later by Marine Brigadier General R. I. Neal, a principal spokesman for the U.S. command in Saudi Arabia during the Persian Gulf War.[12] The press, Neal told a group of editors, never asked the difficult questions for which he had spent four or five hours preparing each day during the war.

Thus, ignorance and inexperience on the part of the mass Persian Gulf press corps protected and supported the Army establishment's determination to keep its aviators in a "support" role. In the months following the war the Army's top leadership exploited that same ignorance and inexperience to protect its "crown jewels": funding for a new "family" of armored vehicles, retention of a parachute division that had once again proven useless as such in major combat operations, and maintenance of a heavy armored corps in Germany.

In his post-victory congratulatory message to the Army, General Carl Vuono, nearing the end of his tenure as Army chief of staff, never so much as mentioned the historic, spectacular success of the 101st Airborne Division and the other combat aviation units. The AH–64 was listed as just one of an inventory of successful Army weapons. "This war was fought and won," said General Vuono, "by armored forces, by light forces . . . and by our sister services and our coalition partners."[13]

When Senator William S. Cohen (R–Me.) wrote to the Army on behalf of a constituent to inquire about the implications of the air cavalry successes, he was sent an article cleverly crafted to focus on the aviation elements of the 24th Mechanized Division in a "support" role, never so much as mentioning the 101st Airborne Division and the French.[14]

In an address to the U.S. Army Armor Association a few weeks later, Vuono continued to build the smokescreen. "Beginning with the arrival of the first [60-ton] Abrams tanks in those early, uncertain days of the crisis," Vuono told his appreciative audience, "the United States and our coalition partners methodically built a mighty force that could withstand the power of the Iraqi Army."[15] The fact that most of those Abrams tanks were unloaded under the protection of a covering force of American and French attack helicopters and that the heavy armor never got closer than seven hours behind the attack helicopters were simply ignored.

In the bureaucratically safe interval between the retirement of General Vuono and the accession of a successor who would prove equally committed to the status quo, Major General Rudolph Ostovich III, departing from his assignment as chief of Army aviation, conveyed to Sean Naylor of *Army Times* what more junior Army aviators had been saying for months to any journalist who would listen to them: The attack helicopter is taking the place of the tank as the centerpiece of land warfare.[16]

All of that went over the heads of the Washington press corps. The Army status quo had weathered the storm.

On another occasion in the 1960s, walking back down the Pentagon's E

Ring corridor toward his office from a Department of Defense news conference, a senior public affairs officer related to the author that "Dealing with the press is like going on a date with a gorgeous idiot girl. You've got to exercise a great deal of restraint." The military services and the Defense Department do not always exercise such restraint.

On July 2, 1991, the chiefs of seventeen major U.S. news organizations sent a report to the Secretary of Defense bemoaning the restrictions imposed on press coverage during the Persian Gulf War.[17] Yet it was clear from the record of the preceding months that even with all of the relevant information before it, the press was unable to make an accurate assessment of what had occurred. Why, then, should journalists utterly ignorant and inexperienced in the history, language, organization, methods, and technology of the subject they are covering, when that subject has a bearing on the life or death of thousands (indeed, of an entire nation), be permitted to roam about at will and to report without effective supervision?

NOTES

1. William V. Kennedy, "The War Fought One Foot Above the Ground," *The National Guardsman* (July 1960): 4–5, 26–28.

2. Ferdinand M. von Senger und Etterlin, "New Operational Concepts," *Journal of the Royal United Service Institute for Defence Studies* (London) (June 1983): 11–15.

3. Richard E. Simpkin, *Race to the Swift* (London: 1985). Brassey's Defence Publishers. The recommendation appears on page 128 in a chapter entitled "The Rotary Wing Revolution," a thoughtful analysis developing many of General von Senger und Etterlin's themes.

4. "Gazelle de sables: Des helicopteres . . . mais surtout des hommes," *Armees D'Aujourd'hui* (Ministry of Defense, Paris) 161 (June–July 1991): 82–84.

5. "What to Deploy" (Opinion), *Christian Science Monitor*, 20 August 1990.

6. "Only a Helicopter Cavalry Can Beat Armored Iraqis" (Viewpoints), *Newsday*, 31 August 1990.

7. The description of air cavalry operations that follows is based on briefings by the U.S. XVIII Airborne Corps and the 101st Airborne Division (Air Assault), July 1991; verbatim after-action debriefings of attack helicopter battalion commanders; summaries of unit staff journals; and interviews with major participants. The 24th Mechanized Division did not reply to an offer to discuss the evidence presented in the foregoing research that it performed a follow-on role to the air cavalry, rather than the lead role ascribed to it in Department of the Army pronouncements, notably the nationally broadcast script read during the post-war Washington victory parade.

8. U.S. Congress, Congressional Budget Office, *Rapid Deployment Forces: Policy and Budgetary Implications* February 1983.

9. "Military Strategy Overextends U.S." (Opinion), *Philadelphia Inquirer*, 17 October 1983.

10. "When the Best Defense Is a Smokescreen" (Viewpoints), *Newsday*, 3 May 1990.

11. Richard Mackenzie, "Apache Attack," *Air Force* 74 (October 1991): 54–60.

12. John Miller and Fred Schultz, "Interview with Lt. Gen. T. W. Kelly, USA (Ret.)," *U.S. Naval Institute Proceedings* 117 (September 1991): 76.

13. Carl Vuono, "Military Might, Skilled Army Won This War," *Army Times*, 18 March 1991, p. 23.

14. David S. Harvey, "In Battle with the 24th's Aviation Brigade," *Rotor & Wing International* (June 1991): 61–65.

15. Carl Vuono, "Armor and the Future Army: The Challenges of Change and Continuity," *Armor* 100 (May–June 1991): 28–29.

16. Sean D. Naylor, "Tomorrow's Tank," *Army Times*, 5 August 1991, p. 24.

17. Jason DeParle, "17 News Executives Criticize U.S. for 'Censorship' of Gulf Coverage," *New York Times*, 3 July 1991, p. A4.

2

The Roots of Conflict

In general, the people who are attracted to a military career and the people who are attracted to a journalism career don't much like each other.

Patriotism—defined in terms of Stephen Decatur's toast, "Our country, right or wrong,"—is the bedrock of the American military ethos. That is often reinforced by strong religious beliefs. The nature of the work attracts people with an orientation toward athletics and the outdoors and a tendency to prefer the certainties of science and mathematics to the abstractions of literature and philosophy. Fastidiousness in personal appearance and house-keeping is the essential response to group living in peace and war and to the inhuman conditions of the trench and the foxhole. All these are fairly common hallmarks of the career military and of the deeply committed citizen-soldier, -sailor, and -Marine of the National Guard and Reserve as well.[1]

Skepticism—indeed, often hostility and ridicule—toward religion, patriotism, and authority in general has become the hallmark of the twentieth-century journalist. At least among American journalists, there is a tendency to avoid mathematics and science in favor of the abstractions and fantasies of literature, sociology, and political "science." A dislike for any sort of "regimentation" is often expressed by a deliberately cultivated lack of fastidiousness in matters of dress and personal appearance. These character-istics—in particular the ridicule of patriotism—are found frequently enough among journalists to create a stereotype detested by the military.[2]

Even among the exceptions on both sides many of the common traits hold true.

Ulysses S. Grant looked like a bum, cared not in the least what anyone thought of that, and published in his *Memoirs* one of the most scathing denunciations ever written of people who choose the military as a career.

Yet all of that disguised superb horsemanship, an attention to the funda-
mentals of military education and training that gave him an instinctive grasp
of the military situation at all levels from tactical to strategic, and an ability
to infuse an army with a relentless determination, even in the face of horrific
losses, that ranks him with the great captains of history.

The late Keyes Beech, long-time distinguished Asian correspondent for
the former *Chicago Daily News* and later for the *Los Angeles Times*, looked
to the end of his days very much like the young Marine who had gone ashore
at Iwo Jima, and to anyone who has spent much time around the Marines
it was plain that he shared their values and standards. Yet he was severely
critical of the military during the Korean War, and he had a tough-minded
view of authority, expressed in his rule of thumb, "I'll have a drink, but I
won't go upstairs."

By far the greater source of misunderstanding and outright dislike between
the two groups, however, lies in the realm of responsibility.

As early as the age of eighteen, in the case of enlisted members selected
to become non-commissioned officers, and twenty-one or so in the case of
commissioned officers, service members are assigned responsibilities for life,
property, and mission accomplishment that most civilians never encounter
in a lifetime. Very quickly with those responsibilities comes a knowledge of
how easily things can go wrong and of the price to be paid for mistakes,
often in terms of human life and limb.

Journalists, by and large, do not acquire anything approaching comparable
responsibilities until they become editors, broadcast news directors, or television producers much later in their careers, and almost never does that
involve a sense of personal responsibility in matters of life or death. That
lack of experience with responsibility is compounded by the policies of many
journalistic enterprises that prohibit their employees from participating in
local politics or other forms of community action lest a conflict of interest
develop.

"Well then," said a bright young journalist on his first military assignment
when told of how military policy can sometimes evolve from a chain of
accidents, "we are governed by idiots!" Not idiots. Only fallible human
beings. And there was no way to explain to the young reporter how such
facile journalistic criticism, often becoming ridicule, can burn itself into the
soul of its victims.

The end result of this mutual antagonism was summed up by Fred Reed,
one of a rare brand of journalists who have sought to develop an expertise
in military affairs and to report such "without fear or favor." "I do a lot of
magazine writing," Reed wrote. "I know that I can easily sell articles criticizing the military, but that a piece praising anything the services do is
nearly impossible to peddle. In conversation, magazine editors almost without exception are hostile and contemptuous of the military."[3]

Virtually all of Reed's contemporaries and predecessors except those on the staffs of very narrowly focused defense publications, and for a time Reed himself, were driven from the field of military specialization. This happened in part because most editors are hostile toward anyone who writes favorably of the military, in part because the military itself is not anxious to have knowledgeable reporters looking into its affairs.

The open antagonism between the military and the media has much deeper roots, however. In their report of a study commissioned by the American Society of Newspaper Editors in May 1982 Judee and Michael Burgoon of the University of Michigan found from research among the staffs of eight major newspapers that journalists 'do not have many values or interests in common with the public."[4]

In short, most journalists, at least at the national level, tend to think of the public as a *lumpenproletariat*. Haynes Johnson, one of the *Washington Post's* most senior writers, refers to the public during participation in the weekly public television program "Washington Week in Review" as "Joe Sixpack." Indeed, research by the Burgoons and others indicates that the image of the American public carried by most national print and broadcast journalists is that of the loutish lead in the long-running Norman Lear television series "All in the Family." The subtle identification of that figure as a Catholic also tallies with the findings of virtually every media survey in the past twenty years that most national communications media professionals, journalists as well as television sitcom writers and producers, are strongly anti-religious, with practicing Catholics and Evangelical Protestants the most despised of the lot.

No wonder that reporters covering the Gulf War of 1991 were astonished to find that "this is a mainly God-fearing, patriotic, family-centered Army." The military-media antagonism, then, is the reflection of a much deeper division between the values of the American public and the values of an alienated media elite. Why, then, should journalists have been surprised when they turned to the public for support against military control of the press during the Grenada expedition of 1983, the Panama invasion of 1989, and the Persian Gulf War and encountered only a wave of pro-military, anti-press hostility?

Despite the mutual antagonism, there are enough of the atypical Ulysses Grant and Keyes Beech types to make possible a working relationship if the top management on both sides of the military-media divide can be forced to develop it. To varying degrees the leaders of the U.S. Army, Air Force, and Marine Corps have been willing to make such an effort, with the result that, because there is no countervailing degree of management wisdom and expertise on the part of the press, those three services are now able to control how they are reported in any major military operation.

The ultimate result of that situation will be a public misled by both the military and the press into believing that it is well informed. No one understands that better than do the families of Persian Gulf War casualties who learned that deaths reported to them by the military as caused by enemy fire turned out to have been inflicted by misdirected U.S. fire. They would learn the truth neither from the military nor from the press, but rather from comrades of their loved ones whose consciences would not permit them to remain silent.

The hope for reform lies in a specialized craft of military journalism practiced intermittently and with great difficulty over the past century and a half by no more than a dozen or so people, maximum, at any one time.

Herodotus and Thucydides of Greece created military writing in the West in a form that Julius Ceasar would turn into an instrument of power. Quite a different, and superior form emerged in the East with an analysis of war by the Chinese general Sun Tzu.

The generals and the admirals had the reporting and analysis of war pretty much to themselves until the *London Times* sent William Howard Russell to cover the Crimean War in 1854.[5] Whatever the degree of journalistic competence, things have not been the same for the generals since. The admirals continue to live on in a sort of splendid isolation, but that is an illusion.

Until World War I, the journalists who followed Russell on the battlefield and in the camp produced at least as much misinformation as information, and the quality of their writing in general was equally undistinguished. Perhaps because the level and quality of education of journalists were improving, perhaps because the horrors of the Western Front brought home the fact that war is, indeed, too important to be left to the generals, and the admirals, a small group of journalists began to emerge who understood war in its full scope and who in some individual cases were able to move into competent analysis.

Fletcher Pratt, George Fielding Eliot, Liddell Hart, and, later, Hanson W. Baldwin were prominent members of this group. When Baldwin was hired by the *New York Times* in 1929 as a full-time military reporter, and when the *Baltimore Sun*, the *New York Herald Tribune*, and the *Washington Post* followed suit with Mark Watson, Walter Millis, and John G. Norris, respectively, it seemed that American journalism was about to accord military coverage in peace as well as in war at least a tiny fraction of the status and resources it has traditionally given to sports and what was once known as the "society page."

In several cases the new military specialists were military or journalistic veterans of World War I who had seen as much, or more, of combat as had any U.S. military officer on active duty, and that did much to bridge the gap between the two antagonistic cultures. Although Baldwin was too young to have served in World War I, his credentials as a graduate of the Naval Academy with subsequent active service were impeccable.

The respect and confidence gained among the military high commands by these few, but highly competent, reporters and analysts in the 1920s and

1930s had much to do with the generally excellent working relationship between the U.S. military high command and the press during World War II. An incident during the Sicilian campaign when the great potential of General George S. Patton, Jr. was nearly lost because he slapped an enlisted hospital patient[6] was by no means the only critically important story handled with good judgment and mutual understanding by all parties concerned, without damage to the public interest.

Some of the original group of military specialists were still around when the Korean War broke out in June 1950. There seemed to be good prospects that a younger group of journalists seasoned during the latter phase of World War II and during the bitterly frustrating Korean campaigns would at least replace the aging original group. Among the most promising new prospects were Keyes Beech; Marguerite Higgins who, as a correspondent, had taken the surrender of Dachau in World War II and who had gone on to win a Pulitzer Prize for combat reporting in Korea; and a photo-journalist, Dickey Chapelle.

That was not the way things turned out. With the exception of Mark Watson of the *Baltimore Sun* and John G. Norris of the *Washington Post* the original group of military specialists was never replaced by reporters of equal competence and equal dedication to the military "beat." The reason why would become evident to anyone who applied for the job.

The managing editor of the *Philadelphia Evening Bulletin*, then considered to be among the elite of American newspapers, told the author as an aspiring military specialist, "I can give you a job, and we'll send you out on military stories when one comes up, but the rest of the time you'll have to do whatever comes along." Even the most cursory review of what the *Bulletin* was publishing as a "military story" would show that anything beyond a change of command ceremony at the Philadelphia Navy Yard was taken off the Associated Press wire. The price of doing "whatever comes along" would be loss of contact with the military, inability to keep up with the current military literature, and, ultimately, retrogression to the abysmal level of ignorance in defense matters that characterized even the best of the national general assignment reporters.

The executive editor of the *Louisville Courier-Journal* felt that he could justify publishing no less than six nationally syndicated columns offering "the broadest possible spectrum of political thought. But when we get to [national defense] I . . . cannot see our newspapers presenting *any* kind" of regular commentary. This editor, one of the most respected in the country, felt that to do so would be to open the way to demands for similar treatment by private pilots, lawyers, florists, and so on.[7]

The managing editor of the equally prestigious *Milwaukee Journal* said essentially that when the paper wanted something from a military specialist, they would run something by Baldwin of the *Times*.[8]

This was at a time, in the late 1950s, when those three newspapers were considered by all journalistic authorities to represent the very best of American journalism. It was also at a time when the echoes of the guns from one major war, in Korea, had scarcely died out; when the guns of another, in Vietnam, were already being heard; and when the world had come to teeter on a nuclear razor's edge with two massive, nuclear-armed armies confronting each other in central Europe.

The managing editor of the *Courier-Journal* could not distinguish between the issues that were important to the Kentucky florists and those that, over the next decade, would kill 58,000 of his countrymen and put at risk all the others. No less astonishing was the ready admission by the *Milwaukee Journal* editor that not only his newspaper, but also every major regional newspaper in the United States of comparable standing relied on one reporter and analyst for national coverage of a story that, in the increasingly perilous nuclear age, was of daily, literally life-or-death importance to its readers.

Thus, by the time the United States began to send military advisers to South Vietnam, in 1961, all that was left of the group of full-time military specialists that had shown so much promise in the 1920s, 1930s, and 1940s had been reduced to a few aging survivors. The consequences of destroying by neglect—or, in the case of the *New York Times*, by deliberate intent—the basis for the good working relationship with the military that had existed during World War II and Korea would open during the Vietnam War a gaping, and still festering, wound. To understand the seriousness of that wound and its implications for the entire American body politic it is necessary to understand that the structural defects in American journalism that would be exposed so dramatically in Vietnam had been evident in the reporting of every major military story since World War II.

NOTES

1. Morris Janowitz, *The Professional Soldier*, (Glencoe, Ill.: Free Press, 1960). This remains the basic text on the subject, essentially reaffirmed by all subsequent research, but dealing only with the regular, career officer.

2. There is a large body of research on the subject, all of it affirming the characteristics described. See, inter alia, Stephen Hess, *The Washington Reporters* (Washington, D.C.: Brookings Institution, 1981); Ernest W. Lefever, *TV and National Defense: An analysis of CBS News, 1972–73* (Boston, Va.: Institute for American Strategy, 1974); S. Robert Lichter, Stanley Rothman, and Linda S. Lichter, *The Media Elite* (Bethesda, Md.: Adler and Adler, 1986).

3. Fred Reed, "Press vs. Military: A Recipe for Conflict," *Army Times*, 18 May 1987, p. 78. The same sort of experience is reported by Richard Halloran, former defense correspondent of the *New York Times*: "I [had] little problem getting stories about incompetent soldiers into the paper, but I have had trouble getting into print [favorable stories]. . . . Stories about soldiers embezzling money get into the paper faster, and are played better, than stories about the plummeting rate of drug abuse

in the armed forces; the list is nearly endless." (Lecture presented at the Center for Defense Journalism, Boston University, 7 May 1988).

4. Paraphrased by Jonathan Friendly, "Reporter's Notebook: Insiders on Journalism," *New York Times*, 8 May 1982, p. 8.

5. For historical development, see John Hohenberg, *Foreign Correspondence: The Great Reporters and Their Times* (New York: Columbia University, 1964); Phillip Knightley, *The First Casualty: From the Crimea to Vietnam* (New York: Harcourt Brace, 1975).

6. Ladislas Farago, *Patton: Ordeal and Triumph* (New York: Obolensky, 1963), chaps. 16 and 17.

7. Norman E. Isaacs in correspondence with author, May–June 1963.

8. Orville Schaleben in correspondence with author, June 1961 to December 1962.

3

Television: The Here, Now, and Obituary Medium

There is a scene toward the end of the 1950s British movie *Darling* in which the flamed-out lover is driving his erstwhile mistress to the airport for a final farewell.

"You've got to admit," she says, "that I was the most important part of your life."
Gazing glumly over the steering wheel, he replies, "It was certainly the most dramatic."

Ask any television news executive what role the medium plays in American journalism, and he or she will pull out surveys showing that the greater part of the American public long ago came to depend primarily, and probably in most cases entirely, on television. "More people get their news from ABC than from any other source," ABC News proudly boasts. But what do they get?

Drama? Certainly, that's what the ratings competition among the networks is all about. Emotion? The viewer is fairly bathed in it.

Understanding? Above all, the sort of understanding that enables people to plan their lives to avoid danger *before* a crisis is upon them or to seize an opportunity?

It is fair to say that the United States was committed to a major war in the Persian Gulf in August 1991—well before the majority of the American public understood the issue. Certainly the public did not know that, for a period of time, only the use of nuclear weapons could assure the safety of U.S. national interests and military personnel involved in an operation that was a result of unilateral presidential decisions and actions. It is also fair to say that, by the time the U.S. Congress got around to voting to legitimize the presidential actions, the degree to which the national interest and the lives of large numbers of Americans had been committed made it impossible to do otherwise than rubber-stamp the president's actions.

If neither the public nor the Congress understood what was happening during the crucial early days and weeks when the nation was being committed irrevocably to war, what does that say of what the public freely acknowledges to be its primary source of news and of what is—in fact, if not so readily acknowledged—also the primary source of national and international news for most members of the Congress?

During and immediately after the Persian Gulf War of 1991 all of those questions concerning the adequacy and competence of television journalism came to be personified in the role that Peter Arnett of the Cable News Network (CNN) played as an on-the-scene reporter in Baghdad when that city came under allied bombardment. There was drama aplenty as Arnett and his CNN colleagues reported the first U.S. Navy Tomahawk missile to strike Baghdad and provided first-hand accounts of the allied bombardment thereafter. Even the chairman of the U.S. Joint Chiefs of Staff would acknowledge being thrilled by those eyewitness, here-and-now accounts.

But all that is shattered by a question of understanding. Was it truly a bomb shelter to which Arnett and his cameraman were led by Iraqi officials to view the horror of hundreds of civilian dead? Or was it an Iraqi command post, as claimed by the allied high command? or was it both, used as a command post during daylight and as a civilian bomb shelter at night? Bomb shelters, the allied command would argue, are not ordinarily surrounded by barbed wire and topped by communications antennae.

Whatever the truth, unknowable in the absence of a thorough, independent on-the-scene investigation, the Arnett reports undoubtedly brought into question the allied claim that it was seeking to avoid civilian casualties. And that reinforced anti-allied sentiment among Arab populations throughout the Middle East and anti-war sentiment within the United States.

The Arnett reports gave the Iraqis a powerful instrument of propaganda. An Iraqi regime that could claim to have survived an onslaught by almost all of the world's major nations could conceivably put the Arnett reports to more effective use in the long term than it was able to do during the war itself. Indeed, it is not difficult to picture tapes of the Arnett reports of the catastrophe being played before sympathetic Arab audiences throughout the Middle East. That is what any professional U.S. public relations firm would have done for a client, and the Iraqis have demonstrated that they are fully acquainted with Western public relations techniques.

Had the reports by Arnett and other CNN correspondents in Baghdad produced drama? Indeed, with huge economic benefits to CNN worldwide.

Had those reports produced understanding? Far from it. Months after the fighting was ended and he was safe back in Washington, Arnett himself would still be defending his identification of a bomb-damaged building as a "milk powder factory," as a crudely lettered Iraqi sign had labeled it, in English.

So the end product of the CNN Baghdad reporting was not understanding. Rather, it was an inflaming of bitterness on the part of Arabs already convinced that the United States as Israel's principal sponsor and benefactor is a mortal foe and on the part of Americans who cheered on the allied forces in the Gulf War and who bitterly resented the cloud cast over their efforts by the Arnett reporting.

How bitter the reaction was on the part of at least some Americans was revealed on February 20, 1991, when, in testimony before the Senate Committee on Governmental Affairs, retired U.S. Army Colonel Harry G. Summers, Jr., denounced Arnett and his other CNN Baghdad colleagues for having "given aid and comfort to the enemy."[1] Later, in his weekly nationally distributed Los Angeles Times News Service column, Summers accused Arnett of "treason."[2] Because treason is a crime punishable by death in time of war, those were the most serious charges any American could lodge against a countryman. Indeed, they were without precedent in terms of charges made by one member of the journalistic establishment against another.

In a later Los Angeles Times News Service commentary Summers would conclude that Arnett was not a traitor. Rather, he was only a "toady" who, as a New Zealander by birth," leaned over backwards to demonstrate his lack of bias in favor of his adopted country" to please a network owner who sees himself as a "world journalist."[3]

Summers at that time routinely identified himself as a "Distinguished Fellow of the U.S. Army War College," and there were no demurrers from the Army or anyone else in high authority. Arnett's defenders came solely and entirely from within the media. The lack of any sort of defense for Arnett from the public at large should have been seen by the press as one more ominous signal of a sullen and growing hostility, but it was not.

Sadly, the entire episode could have been avoided if the press had understood the implications of issues examined in detail three years before the Gulf War under the aegis of the Columbia University Seminars on Media and Society and broadcast over Public Television.[4] In a segment titled "Under Orders, under Fire," Harvard Law School Professor Charles Ogletree led a panel of distinguished representatives from the military, the press, church groups, Congress, and the general public through a series of excruciating moral dilemmas.

To ABC News anchorman Peter Jennings, Ogletree offered the hypothetical opportunity to go behind enemy lines and to accept the offer of an enemy of the United States to see for himself proof of atrocities by a U.S. ally. And then, while accompanying an enemy patrol, it was posited that Jennings would find himself in the middle of preparations for the ambush of a unit of the U.S. ally accompanied by American advisers. Would he warn the Americans?

After visibly agonizing with himself, Jennings responded with "what I'm feeling . . . I would do what I could to warn the Americans even though it would cost me my life. Others might have a different view."

"Others would have a different view," Mike Wallace of CBS News responded. "They would regard it simply as another story that they are there to cover."

"Do you see no higher duty,"Ogletree asked, "as an American citizen?"

"No," Wallace replied, "you don't have a higher duty."

"I chickened out," Jennings interjected. "I think Mike is right."

Retired Air Force Lieutenant General Brent Scowcroft, later national security adviser to President George Bush, asked Wallace and Jennings to weigh a thirty-second film clip against the lives of U.S. soldiers.

"I'm going back and forth as I sit here," Wallace replied. "I don't know," but he acknowledged that he had long since determined that, warned of an impending murder in a U.S. city, he would do what he could to warn the intended victim, rather than exploit the information for its journalistic value.

General William C. Westmoreland, commander of the U.S. forces during the Vietnam War, observed that, if confronted with the death of Americans filmed by an American television crew that could have warned the Americans, the U.S. public would conclude "that the press is in cahoots with the enemy."

"And what do you feel?" Ogletree asked Marine Colonel George M. Connell.

"I feel utter contempt. Two days later those same two journalists are caught in an ambush and are lying wounded 200 yards from my positions, and they expect that I'm going to send Marines to get them.

"They're not Americans. They're just journalists.

"You can't have it both ways.

"But I'm going to go after them, and Marines will die going to get a couple of journalists.

"And that's what makes me so contemptuous of them."

Wallace's initial reaction was bitterly condemned in veterans' magazines and elsewhere. When the author asked by letter in 1991 if his views were being reported correctly in those condemnatory articles, Wallace responded immediately, by telephone.

"As you will see from the tape," Wallace said, "I responded without having had time to think about the subject, and immediately began to have second thoughts.

"I am an American. I fought for our country in World War II as a member of the U.S. Naval Reserve. I am not going to see American fighting men and women killed or injured if there is anything I can do to stop it. But having had a lot of time to think about that question, I don't think it can be addressed outside of the much larger question of whether the press should seek to get people behind enemy lines in time of war. Once you are in there, in enemy territory, you are no longer a free agent. You are under enemy control. You could find yourself in the situation Charles Ogletree painted at any moment. Aside from questions of legality, the press has got to ask itself whether it should make the attempt at all to get an enemy government to grant access."

Does that not relate, Wallace was asked, to the trip by Harrison Salisbury of the *New York Times* to Hanoi during the Vietnam War? Didn't that put Salisbury just a step away from the situation posited to Jennings?

"Exactly," Wallace replied.

The press routinely castigates the U.S. government for "failures of Intelligence." Yet here was a classic warning, fully developed in an ideal academic environment and broadcast nationwide. By continuing to operate behind enemy lines in time of war the journalists involved would be at any moment only a step away from the disastrous situation portrayed by Ogletree. If that situation were to materialize, the public outrage described by General Westmoreland and Colonel Connell could lead to permanent damage to First Amendment rights.

At no point during or after the Persian Gulf War was there the slightest indication that the management of CNN, or of any other news organization, print or broadcast, had absorbed the warning and fully understood its implications. Arnett and his colleagues were posted in Baghdad and kept there solely and entirely for commercial advantage, an advantage from which CNN reaped huge immediate financial rewards. The long-term costs of a growing public perception that the press will not hesitate to make whatever pacts with an enemy of the United States it deems useful and profitable are yet to be calculated.

Is Arnett, therefore, a "traitor," as Colonel Summers stated in his initial condemnation? Or only a slightly less contemptible "toady"? Neither. Something more frightening, and more dangerous.

In agreeing to report from Baghdad after the start of hostilities, Peter Arnett had become the mere extension of a camera lens, endowing that lens with a voice and to that degree dehumanizing himself. Permitted only to photograph the bombed shelter, the camera showed but one more scene of human carnage and property damage, identical to the endless chain of such scenes that are the hallmark of the twentieth century. It was Arnett's voice and presence that gave the scene whatever meaning it possessed. Yet it was not, as Mike Wallace noted, the voice and presence of a free agent.

By shaping, in toto, the circumstances by which Arnett would be able to investigate and report, the Iraqi government controlled both the short-term and the long-term impressions and messages of the CNN report. Coming straight from the Iraqi government, the intended message would have been dismissed out of hand by anyone not actively seeking confirmation of prejudgments about the motives, methods, and veracity of the allies. Broadcast worldwide by CNN, the Baghdad reports were clothed in a false aura of journalistic objectivity and reliability.

To permit oneself to be placed in a situation wherein intellect can be expanded or contracted by an external controlling hand, exactly as the lens of a camera is adjusted to the available light, is, indeed, to be dehumanized. That supremacy of technology over human understanding and control is the central flaw of television and of broadcast news in general.

The suppression and the distortion of the intellectual component of broadcast news derive not only from technology, but also from outdated concepts of organization and training and from false values imposed by management.

Dating from the time he joined CBS News in 1935, Edward R. Murrow is deemed by virtually all broadcasters to be the founder of modern broadcast journalism. Yet at no point in his career did Murrow have either the time or the supporting staff required to go beyond what was happening at the moment or what had happened—in short, here-and-now and obituary journalism. As measured by the "O'Sullivan Rule," cited on the dedication page, broadcast news from Murrow's days to this would be the medium that could tell the drowning man that the dam had broken or record in vivid color his obituary—nothing more.

The reporting that made Murrow famous was his gripping, here-and-now coverage of the Battle of Britain for CBS News. We could hear the sirens, the roar of the anti-aircraft batteries, the crash of the bombs; we could feel to at least some degree the sufferings of the victims. From that day to this such here-and-now reporting has been the strength and the mainstay of broadcast journalism, at least as practiced by the major commercial television networks.

Murrow hired a man who was equipped to move beyond the here-and-now into competent analysis. William L. Shirer was a reporter trained in the realm of "print"—newspaper, magazine, book—journalism, and he had made himself a specialist in European politics.

Murrow, CBS manager for all of Europe, had concluded, in Shirer's words, that "he could not cover all of Europe from London." Even Shirer does not seem to have comprehended the stupefying naïveté of the notion that the problem could be resolved by hiring one more broadcast journalist.

"I have a job," Shirer recorded in his diary following his interview with Murrow, "*if* my voice is all right."[5] It would require a corporate decision in New York, based not on journalistic competence, but on the modulations of voice, to put on the air the one reporter in broadcast history whose grasp of the political situation, founded in years of specialized study of a particular region, would provide warning of approaching catastrophe in time for the listener to make intelligent decisions.

A rasping voice, or a distinct American regional accent, would have obviated all of Shirer's study, training, and experience. That has been the norm in broadcast journalism from that day to this, increased enormously in intensity when television brought appearance and all other aspects of personality as well as voice into the equation.

What is it about the nature of the principal commercial networks that so inverts the journalistic sense of values? As seen by Everette E. Dennis, executive director of the Gannett Center for Media Studies at Columbia University, "Broadcasters are storytellers, newspapers are fact gatherers and organizers of information, and news magazines are a hybrid of both."[6] More broadly stated, the broadcast industry was founded to entertain, not to inform, and therein lies its most profound difference from the print medium.

That is not to say that newspapers and the news magazines do not seek to entertain or that they are always competent and reliable sources of information. But their intent, their reason for being is to inform, and that at least establishes a standard totally different from that under which commercial broadcast journalism has operated throughout its history.

To examine the history of journalism as practiced by the three major commercial networks—ABC, NBC, and CBS—during the past twenty-five years is to take note of a pattern of decline identical in all three cases and clearly exposing the weaknesses inherent in any news operation conducted as an adjunct to entertainment. In all cases the network news staffs were assembled mainly from among print journalists trained in the nineteenth-century tradition of the "city room"—that is, a newsroom filled essentially with generalists, mainly liberal arts graduates, sent to cover an infinite variety of stories by other generalists who had graduated to the periphery of the "city desk" as subeditors, all supervised by a city editor who sat in "The Slot."

Whatever else has changed in network journalism, the city-room organizational model based on the supposed omniscience of the general assignment reporter remains inviolable because it is the cheapest way to operate.

Local and regional stations could get along reasonably well with the city-room concept. By carefully reading the daily newspaper the generalists of the local and, to a lesser degree, the regional broadcast news staffs could stay reasonably well informed of ongoing stories, and by monitoring the police, fire, and ambulance radio nets they could be alerted to fast-breaking events. Even so, the rapid turnover of news personalities that has characterized the local and regional broadcast business from the start mostly precludes analysis of trends with any degree of competence. Only rarely would a local broadcast news personality stay around long enough to develop the experience and sources that are the bread and butter of the print journalist.

There has been a great deal more continuity at the national level, initially based on such print-trained journalists as Walter Cronkite, Howard K. Smith, and Harry Reasoner. As they retired or died, however, they were replaced by the products of the "happy-talk" local and regional news "shows." Just as the quality of William L. Shirer's voice was more important to the

New York network executives than were his journalistic talents and his background, so good looks as well as a pleasing voice now became the primary criteria for selection and retention. Indeed, some of the latter generation "stars" of the national broadcast news have proclaimed themselves so lacking in the most basic of all journalistic skills that they have hired "ghosts" to write their 'autobiographies."

The fading away of the old print-trained "stars" in the mid–1980s was accompanied by a management emphasis on entertainment even more pronounced than had been apparent from the beginning. As described by one long time producer at NBC, "The management of the networks takes the view that news is a product . . . whose growth rate has slowed."[7] "Growth" (i.e., profits) lay in entertainment and sports, so there began a drastic reduction in what little expertise the networks had built up in any specialized journalistic field, symbolized by the dismissal, in 1985, of Fred Graham, the seasoned CBS Supreme Court and law correspondent. Even more damaging has been the steady reduction in the research staffs, pruned ruthlessly to sustain the extravagant salaries paid to the on-the-air "stars."

Given limitations on that scale, you might think the new stars would be careful to confine themselves to demonstrable fact. Not so. Virtually every news report on the major commercial television networks is a blend of fact, analysis, and opinion, but without the sharp dividing lines print journalism makes by physically separating what it claims to be objective reporting from analysis and opinion labeled as such. Thus, in a report from Moscow on August 23, 1991, CBS's Jonathan Sanders, solemnly introduced by anchorman Dan Rather as a "Soviet scholar," went from reporting the situation following an attempted coup d'etat earlier in the month to analysis of where the situation was likely to go in the future to condemnation of U.S. President George Bush for having appointed a new ambassador, Robert Strauss, who, in the opinion of the "Soviet scholar," lacked the necessary expertise. All this in about a minute.

The viewer would not be enlightened then, or ever, as to the credentials of the "Soviet scholar" other than his evident ability to speak well, in English, before a camera. Does he speak and read Russian? Has he read deeply into Russian history? Had he traveled the length and breadth of the old Soviet empire in developing his analysis of things to come? Or was he basing those profundities on chatter he had picked up around Moscow? And what would become of the "Soviet scholar" if and when Russia dropped from the drama of day-to-day news? Transferred to, say, Buenos Aires, would he then become a "Latin American scholar"? Intriguing thought to anyone familiar with the pattern of network news management.

On December 26, 1991, Tom Fenton—like Murrow, CBS correspondent for Europe, all the way from the Atlantic to the Urals—would turn a report on the nascent Ukrainian army into ridicule of the notion of the Ukrainians ever embarking on such a venture. Alluding to unnamed U.S. government authorities who apparently planted that idea in his mind, Fenton skillfully employed embarrassing camera shots of the struggling new army to reinforce his words. Fenton ignored the existence of animosities between the Ukraine and Russia deriving from hundreds of years of history. He did not even so much as mention the fact that as recently as the 1950s the United States had supported with agents and arms a Ukrainian nationalist uprising designed to bring about the very independence, army included, Fenton was ridiculing; apparently the U.S. government "authorities" were also unaware of these events. Yet the viewer was expected to accept it all—"shaped" photography, opinion, and profound judgments based on questionable sources—as "news."

Why this sort of thing happens is evident from the policy expressed by Roone Arledge, president of ABC News, in explaining yet another of the news staff reductions of the 1970s and 1980s: "Regarding the layoffs in London, which will lose more than 20 of its staff members, Mr. Arledge said, 'Our needs have changed. We still have a major emphasis on foreign news but there is not as much news out of Europe as there was for awhile. If it happened that more coverage were needed again we would staff back up.' "[8]

Properly trained and left in place, might some of those twenty have hit on the fact that the United States was maintaining far larger forces in Europe than were necessary, given the maturing of the West German army and the obvious weaknesses in the Soviet army? At least as early as 1980 that had become apparent to specialists in military affairs.[9] It never got through to the American public at large. No one in the television news divisions upon whom the public, and Congress, depend for most of their news had the self-confidence born of many years on the specialized defense news "beat" to defy the entrenched service interests that depended on those excessive garrisons for promotions and all the other emoluments of bureaucratic structure.

Properly trained and left in place, might a few of those twenty have begun to understand, as had the members of the highly specialized staffs of Radio Liberty and Radio Free Europe,[10] that the entire structure of the Soviet Union was weakening? Properly reported when the weaknesses were becoming apparent, that information could have led to the saving of at least a part of the extravagantly excessive defense expenditures of the Reagan administration.

And when events compelled Arledge to "staff back up," would all those hired be trained in the background of the new events, or would they be recruited from among people engaged in covering everything from dog shows to the latest scandals of the British royal family? Subsequent experience would show that the broadcast networks would not "staff back up" in terms of hiring or rehiring Americans. Instead, they would increasingly rely on two international corporations, Visnews, Ltd., and Worldwide News Corporation, based in London, staffed by non–U.S. nationals and engaged in producing corporate promotional videos as well as news, but, obviously, not news that might embarrass corporate customers.[11] But their products are reported by the networks to the U.S. public as though coming from what are presumably U.S.-owned and -staffed news organizations. These are the same news organizations that are demanding they be granted unlimited access to the U.S. armed forces in time of war and the right to transmit instantly and without official review or restraint the information gathered to enemy as well as U.S. audiences.

Dan Rather of CBS vociferously defends continued dependence on continental-scope general assignment reporters against the notion that a country such as Japan or Germany demands highly specialized training and attention. Yet, as the introduction of the "Soviet scholar" indicates, Rather himself does not really believe that. Together with the "anchors" of ABC and NBC, he knows he has no other choice. The economics of the networks have deprived him even of specialized expertise in the relatively low paid, and diminishing, research staffs, let alone in terms of the extravagantly paid on-camera "reporter-analyst-pundit" types.

For all their public assertions as to the continued validity of general assignment journalism at the national and international levels, the networks are hypersensitive to inquiries about the gutting of the research staffs and the disappearance of such scant staff expertise as ever existed in complex, specialized subject areas. None, including CNN, replied to written requests for identification of full-time research support for network Pentagon television correspondents. Yet the same networks demand that the Department of Defense respond within twenty-four hours, at considerable public expense, to their written or unwritten requests for information.

Asked during a U.S. Army study of press coverage of the military to provide biographies stating the professional background of 16 network reporters who had at various times covered the Pentagon and the Vietnam War, William J. Small, then Senior Vice President and Director of News of CBS, responded with a savage letter—copy to the Secretary of the Army.[12] "If you think you can learn anything from a company biography," Small wrote, "you have no business doing research of any kind." He did not provide the requested biographies.

In an address at the Columbia University School of Journalism in February 1966, David Brinkley, then NBC Washington correspondent, thought he saw a brighter future.

"It might be all right for a program like Danny Kaye's or Lucille Ball's to have stars—famous personalities who are discussed and admired in fan magazines and asked for autographs," Brinkley declared, "but when this system is carried over into television coverage of news . . . it is absurd.

"There may have to be one more generation of the star system," Brinkley opined, "but the world and the news of it grow more complex. It all happens faster all the time. People know more and demand to know still more. . . . The time when one man can give it to them is coming to an end.

"In place of the star system," Brinkley predicted, "we will ... report the news the way the newspapers report it. That is, having several different men or many different men, each of them working all day on one kind of news or one story, and then having them, all of them, report on the air whatever they have learned."[13]

Yet today the "star" system is more firmly entrenched than ever. There are far fewer "men [and women] ... working ... on one kind of news or one story."

Rarely in their history, except during time of war, have the three commercial networks assigned more than one person to full-time coverage of the entire worldwide U.S. military establishment. All such "Pentagon correspondents" have been exactly that, assigned to the Pentagon newsroom where their every move can be tracked by a corps of Department of Defense public affairs officials charged with making sure they learn nothing other than what the Department of Defense wants them to learn.

There could be no more artificial or misleading place in which to "cover" the American military establishment. The Pentagon building is a vast factory of policy, nothing else.

The information that goes into the making of that policy has been sorted and distorted many times before it gets to the Pentagon building. Commanders at every echelon are careful to report only that which reflects favorably upon themselves and their commands. By far the worst distortions, however, occur within the building itself. Budgets are the name of the game, and budgets do not expand on the basis of failure. So just about everything is reported as success. And no one has a greater stake in perpetuating the false picture that emerges than do the political appointees who sit at the top of the Pentagon hierarchy.

Some of the military officers who participate in this process of delusion and self-delusion, mostly in the higher grades, have been corrupted by the process. Most of the middle-grade and junior officers have not been corrupted, or at least try to avoid being corrupted, often by trying to avoid assignment to the Pentagon, and that is truer the farther one gets from the banks of the Potomac. But the network "Pentagon correspondents" seldom get to those far reaches, and even when they do, it is within the traveling cocoon of Pentagon surveillance.

Those terrible disabilities might have been overcome, at least somewhat, if the network Pentagon correspondents were assisted by researchers who were free to read, to travel, and to inquire without the pressure of deadlines. As the networks confirm by their silence, there is no such support. What you see on the air of the four or five commercial network correspondents assigned full- or part-time to national defense is the total investment by ABC, CBS, CNN, and NBC in worldwide coverage of U.S. national defense.

But, above all, it is the perpetuation of the city-room organizational concept that cripples any meaningful network coverage of the U.S. military establishment. Most of the television reporters who have covered the Pentagon have never served in the military. That deficiency is compounded by the lack of academic preparation in military affairs and by the failure of networks to budget for extensive travel free of deadline pressures over a long period of time.

In recent years, David Martin of CBS News, Fred Francis of NBC, and Robert Zelnick of ABC have been accorded a longer than usual tenure, and that is reflected on occasion in that most remarkable achievement for a network journalist—the unearthing of stories not previously published in a newspaper. Martin is unique in the history of television's Pentagon coverage in having coauthored a book on defense issues. Yet these three inadequately trained and supported men are today almost the only experienced American journalists on the defense beat among all the mass communications media, print as well as broadcast.

Increasing public dissatisfaction with the direction in which the three original commercial networks were moving led to the formation of a radio and television network whose announced purpose was to subordinate entertainment to "education." However, the Public Broadcasting System (PBS), staffed by veterans and in some cases fugitives from the commercial networks, only established an anemic copy of the old city-room system. As support from government has dwindled and as it has come to depend on increasingly desperate financial appeals to the general public, PBS has come to depend more and more on the British Broadcasting Corporation (BBC).

As with the more or less surreptitious use of foreign journalists to take the place of reduced American staffs in the commercial network news operations, that poses serious questions regarding both U.S. national security and journalistic integrity. The British Broadcasting Corporation is exactly that—an agency of the British government. All employees of the BBC are "vetted"—that is, screened by MI5, the British equivalent of the U.S. FBI, and all British journalists, whether working for the BBC or not, are subject to the Official Secrets Act by which journalists can be jailed for broadcasting anything deemed to be a matter of "national security" by any British civil servant or high elected official. In short, the BBC is a very sophisticated agency of official propaganda, the more so because the British government has been judicious in suppressing or ordering the distortion of information only in what it considers to be the most compelling circumstances. Few in the PBS audience are aware of this degree of foreign control over the news they are receiving, and the managers of PBS have made no attempt to enlighten them.

Although he is at least as often to be found covering such non-military entities as the tobacco industry, one National Public Radio (NPR) newsman, David Malpus, has by dint of private interest and study become a promising defense reporter. He is the only such, however, employed by either NPR or its public television counterpart, including the MacNeil-Lehrer television news staff. While the "MacNeil-Lehrer Newshour" would achieve a long-sought network news goal—a full hour of news and analysis—the thinness of its staff has prevented it from becoming a major news-gathering organization, its primary strength being its interviews.

In "Wall Street Week" with Louis Rukeyser, however, public television can boast the one program anywhere on the screen that possesses both the specialized expertise and the time to cover a complex subject in the depth it deserves. While "MacNeil-Lehrer" provides a vast smorgasbord of information, most of it irrelevant to the viewer's daily life, Rukeyser compresses into one half hour per week essentially all that the television medium can do for those tempted into the treacherous world of the stock market. The program is a model of what could be done in equally complex, and at least equally dangerous, subject areas such as defense, health care, and specialized overseas regional reporting and analysis.

Public television is the last American preserve of the "documentary," the form by which broadcast journalists were supposed to be able to step out of the routine of daily news to address a subject in greater detail. At least in its original form, in the commercial networks, the staffs who produced the documentaries also produced the daily news broadcasts. As such they were recognizable, in terms of both their abilities and their prejudices, to the audience.

Except for those produced by a full-time "Frontline" staff in Boston, all public television documentaries are the product of free-lancers whose abilities, prejudices, and source of funds are unknown and unknowable to the general audience. Over time, however, a pattern of prejudice has become so obvious as to produce a demand that the network, in toto, be shut down.[14] That demand arose mainly because, like its commercial counterparts, public television accords no means of response from the viewer such as are available to the newspaper and magazine reader through letters to the editor, the op-ed page, and the fully balanced "pro and con" format. Unlike the commercial network viewer, however, the viewer offended by the prevailing public television prejudices feels doubly abused by what is perceived to be the misuse of his or her own taxes.

A classic example of the problem resulting from public television dependence on the indirect foreign subsidy provided by the BBC and its imperviousness to criticism from any source was the "Frontline" broadcast of June 13, 1989, "Death of a Terrorist." The subject, Mairead Farrell, an Irish Republican Army (IRA) member killed in an ambush by British Special Air Service members in Gibraltar the previous year, was effectively condemned in the title. Yet the program offered no evidence that Farrell ever had been guilty of anything meeting the U.S. State Department definition of "terrorist" (i.e., one who makes deliberate attacks on innocent persons for a political purpose). A gunman who had killed and wounded mourners at the funeral of Farrell and two other IRA members killed with her was identified in the program as a Protestant, when, in fact, he was a Catholic. There were numerous other errors of fact, betraying a lack of familiarity with the intricate issues underlying the centuries-old opposition to British rule in Ireland. Indeed, "Frontline" felt comfortable enough with the rightness of the British cause to pose its host, Judy Woodruff, in front of the British embassy in Washington.

Even when requested to do so by members of Congress, "Frontline" refused either to acknowledge on the air its obvious errors of fact or to permit a rebuttal. It has followed the same pattern in every report it has done on U.S. national defense, all of them with a strong anti-military slant.

The long-established PBS habit of placing ideology first and facts second finally produced a disaster with a November 1992 story of how a black tank battalion liberated the concentration camps at Dachau and Buchenwald. The "documentary" was plainly intended to heal a widening breach in New York City and elsewhere between African-American and Jewish communities. However laudable the purpose, it developed in subsequent months that the tank battalion had not been anywhere near either camp, as verified by its own morning reports. In March 1993, the sponsoring station, WNET, Channel 13, in New York, asked that other PBS affiliates cease broadcasting the program pending the outcome of an investigation.[15]

Disappointment with the limitations of commercial network news and PBS biases and elitism led to the creation of the first broadcasting network ever established solely for the reporting of news. The Cable News Network (CNN) went on the air on June 1, 1980, as "the nation's only 24-hour-a-day, seven-day-a-week all-news network."[16]

"Interrupting his own running monologue only to spit tobacco juice into a plastic cup," Tony Schwartz of the *New York Times* reported,[17] Ted Turner, the founder of CNN, declared "The [commercial] network nightly news is nothing more than a headline service. . . . Newspapers have traditionally provided the depth that television hasn't, but the fact is newspapers are getting too expensive to produce and deliver. As energy sources run out, trees are becoming more precious. The Cable News Network will deliver a newspaper electronically."

Questions of substance aside, the viewer cannot turn the pages of CNN, at least not yet. He or she must sit there all day and all night listening to the same news over and over again so as to pick up, in between, whatever analysis and features the editors have drummed up, largely off the op-ed pages of various daily newspapers, to fill in the hours.

The declared environmentalist who at least in 1980 saw nothing incongruous about spitting tobacco juice dominates CNN as William Randolph Hearst, Joseph Pulitzer, Adolph Ochs, Colonel Robert R. McCormick, and others dominated the newspapers they created or acquired. In that and in the priority it gives to news over entertainment, Turner and CNN are in the mainstream of traditional American journalism, in contrast to the three original largely faceless, remotely managed commercial networks. And Turner's prejudices are at least on the surface, unlike the subtleties that infect virtually all public television "documentaries," in particular "Frontline," and the BBC-dependent NPR newscasts.

CNN, however, is also structured on the city-room concept. Except in time of war, it covers national defense as do the commercial networks, by assigning one full-time correspondent to the Pentagon, unsupported by full-time research assistants.

With the commercial networks, and without any full-time PBS coverage, that makes a total of four or five full-time television correspondents to cover the armed services, which for the past forty years have averaged 2 million American men and women stationed throughout the world, and to monitor a Defense Department budget running between $200 and $300 billion.

How well this system functions in peace, or at least relative peace, would seem to be a reasonable indicator of how reliably it can be expected to function in time of war. There is a distinct difference between what television news has succeeded at and what it has failed at in routine, peacetime defense coverage.

Acting almost certainly on a contact from one of the aggrieved parties, on January 15, 1992, CBS Pentagon man Jim Stewart got on the "CBS Evening News" with a report that amputees from the previous year's Persian Gulf War were being issued obsolete and inadequate prosthetic devices. It was the sort of human interest story newspaper editors and broadcast news directors dream about, complete with an on-camera statement by a U.S. Army doctor—a full colonel—who declared, in effect, that in the Army's view the amputees were not worth some $5,000 of taxpayer money to obtain state-of-the-art prosthetics. This was followed by film of a heroic amputee's progress in developing rock-climbing skills with the aid of a modern artificial leg purchased with private funds.

To no great surprise, the chairman of the U.S. Joint Chiefs of Staff was apparently found waiting for the CBS Washington bureau door to open the next morning. The doctor was by then nowhere to be found, but, following the chairman's assurances that the best prosthetic devices available would be provided, no matter what, a Medical Corps brigadier general appeared to tell us what the colonel had really meant to say.

The Medical Corps also figured in a grim and as yet unresolved story aired by CBS's "60 Minutes" on January 31, 1983. Members of the armed services who refuse to keep silent about waste, fraud, and corruption, and even breaches of flying safety, are being slapped into psychiatric wards and their lives devastated. All the time that this has been going on, the U.S. government has been waging a worldwide propaganda campaign against the government of the Soviet Union for engaging in exactly the same practice. The practice appears to have been stopped in what was the Soviet Union. It continues in all of the U.S. armed forces, and it is used to intimidate and punish Defense Department civilian whistle-blowers as well.

Such stories represent the best of journalism, but because of their intensely human focus, they are also the easiest stories to understand and to report. The record of broadcast journalism with respect to more complex military issues is uniformly dismal.

The same Jim Stewart who did so well with the amputee story went on the air on February 24, 1992, with a totally garbled story, picked up from *Army Times*, on the failure of U.S. armored forces to close the trap on Iraqi forces in Kuwait. In fact, the armored forces were more than three days behind the U.S. and French air cavalry forces that were in the process of closing the trap when halted by the cease-fire.

Prior to the Gulf War, the same "60 Minutes" staff that did so well with the psychiatric abuse story deeply embarrassed itself with a report of what a disaster the AH–64 Apache attack helicopter would prove to be if ever it had to go to war. As it turned out, of course, the first time the AH–64 went to war, in the Persian Gulf in 1991, it changed the course of military history. Yet all of the deficiencies that led "60 Minutes" to deride the Apache were real enough. There simply was no one on the CBS news staff to tell the writers and producers that such had been the case with every leading-edge weapon and weapons system from the Pennsylvania rifle to the World War I tank. Nor had they any means to know that such people as General von Senger und Etterlin and Brigadier Simpkin had weighed the AH–64's deficiencies against its demonstrated capabilities and were ready to accept the attack helicopter as the future weapon of decision in land warfare.

As concerns another spectacularly successful Gulf War weapons system, Dave Marash of ABC's "20/20" also plunged into dire predictions, stating that the then XM–1 tank would fall victim to "smaller, lighter and more accurate anti-tank weapons" and that in "some place more warlike than [Fort Knox] Kentucky" the necessity to change air filters would fatally expose the crews.[18] Well, even allowing anti-tank weapons another decade to develop, the M–1 swept aside the Iraqi army in Kuwait with such force that the Americans were being criticized by some at home for burying alive the Iraqi gunners operating the "smaller, lighter and more accurate" weapons. Changing the filters proved to be no real problem since by the time it was necessary to change the filters the Americans had swept the battlefield clear of any enemy who could take aim.

It was not that Marash had misrepresented anything. It was simply that, instead of using caution in covering a tank that was barely out of the prototype stage, he had given too great weight to the theories of a civilian research and development chief who simply did not have the military experience to understand a long-standing lesson from World War II: "That Volkstrommer 1 went out with great gusto with his shoulder-fired Panzerfaust to confront the American tanks, but when Volkstrommers 2 and 3 saw what happened to Volkstrommer 1 they ran for their lives."[19] The tank would be overcome in the Arabian and Iraqi desert, not by a stationary system or by tanks of equal mobility, but by a weapons system with vastly superior mobility, superior fire control systems, and long-range firepower.

It is in the inability to form a valid independent judgment about such conflicting views regarding complex defense issues that television journalism strikes out virtually every time it takes bat in hand. At one time or another in the decade previous to the Persian Gulf War every U.S. weapons system that would prove itself in spectacular fashion on the battlefield was ridiculed in this manner by one or another of the television networks, usually on the authority of some civilian in the General Accounting Office or the Department of Defense itself whose facility with numbers was not matched by either practical experience or a familiarity with the history of war.

Bitter and frustrated over such embarrassments, network television lost no time returning to the attack once the Persian Gulf War was over. On January 29, 1992, Lesley Stahl, appearing on CBS's "60 Minutes," entered a warehouse at the New Cumberland, Pennsylvania, Defense Logistics Depot. She was dressed in a manner that probably no more than a dozen women in central Pennsylvania could afford and that was certainly beyond even the dreams of the hundreds of women who worked in that warehouse. An obliging U.S. Army colonel, the depot commander, conducted Stahl to several large boxes, conveniently lined up and opened in advance. There Stahl "discovered" large quantities of surgical gowns which she identified in mock surprise as dating from 1945 and, therefore, as she instructed the audience, not only excess to any conceivable requirement, but also "obsolete."

How obsolete can a surgical gown get? No matter—the audience was told to accept, on Stahl's authority, that there could be no conceivable use for such large quantities of the gowns, obsolete or not. The country had just concluded a war in which the original estimates of U.S. casualties had run to 10,000, almost certainly requiring many boxes of those surgical gowns at New Cumberland, the principal logistics depot supporting U.S. forces throughout Europe and the Middle East. A single Hiroshima-size nuclear warhead among the thousands available to former and potential U.S. enemies exploded over a U.S. city would have exhausted the stocks of surgical gowns at New Cumberland in a matter of hours—and undoubtedly left television news demanding to know why more were not instantly available.

Much was made of the fact that some outrageous sum would be required to package and ship a single flashlight battery from New Cumberland to some overseas destination. Yet no evidence was produced to show that the depot was given to shipping batteries one at a time, nor did the by now totally befuddled colonel or an inept Defense Logistics Agency public affairs office pounce on that patently false issue.

As the clincher, Stahl, still in high fashion, was posed, carefully, amidst a pile of military truck tires, again instructing the audience as to the horrific waste that storage of such a vast number of tires represented. The total sum of the tires visible looked to be about the annual consumption of one heavy truck company among the several score of such companies supported from New Cumberland on a throughput system that allows for no large stocks at intermediate field depots.

It was a hatchet job, done in a manner that made it plain network news had learned nothing from a long and bitter trial following the Vietnam War in which General William C. Westmoreland sued CBS for what the network itself would admit were prejudiced and distorted allegations that General Westmoreland had falsified estimates of enemy strength. Despite the evidence of public hostility toward the press that had been mounting ever since the Grenada invasion of 1983, the producers seemed to have had no comprehension of the residue of hatred such deliberate distortions leave behind, and not only among the military. Once again, in that logistics depot warehouse, an elitist, extravagantly paid, anti-military media had set itself apart from the greater part of the American public—not least of all by the manner in which Stahl dressed and by her expert, contemptuous manipulation of the depot commander, a decent chap with whom the vast majority of the American public would instantly identify.

The nineteenth-century city-room system of organization and its reliance on English, sociology, and political "science" majors simply cannot cope with the pace and the intricacies of twentieth-century, soon to be twenty-first-century, warfare. That is compounded by an emotional mindset to a large extent shaped and deepened by the pitfalls television journalism dug for itself from the 1960s into the 1990s.

" 'We know that unilateral action in Grenada and Tripoli was wrong. We know that Star Wars means uncontrollable escalation of the arms race. . . . We've got to shout these truths . . . from the rooftops.' "[20] So spoke Walter Cronkite in an interview with Jeremy Gerard of the *New York Times* published on January 8, 1989. More than any other man, Cronkite shaped the nature of modern "star"-centered broadcast journalism. That the passionate anti-defense doctrine he proclaimed as unchallengeable "truth" was shared throughout the journalistic community of the 1970s and 1980s is not disputed by anyone on any side of the argument. And it was this that gave a touch of evangelism to such as the network condemnations of the AH–64 helicopter and the M–1 tank.

How could they have been so wrong? It was their sources that misled them.

The news-gathering resources of broadcast journalism, as such, would have difficulty filling 10 percent of the air time currently devoted to news by all of the networks, CNN included. It is the newspapers and the wire services that keep television news on the air, and it is to the newspapers and the wire services that we must look to determine why television news is unable to do more than tell the drowning man that the dam has broken or report his obituary. In the words of one broadcast journalism's own "stars," Ted Koppel, "The network news divisions compete to be first with the obvious."[21]

NOTES

1. U.S. Congress, Senate, Committee on Government Affairs, 20 February 1991 (As broadcast by CSPAN on same date).

2. Harry G. Summers, "Treason, Pure and Simple," *Army Times*, 15 April 1991, p. 62.

3. Harry G. Summers, "Peter Arnett: No Traitor, but a Toady," *Army Times*, 2 December 1991, p. 62.

4. "Media and Society, Ethics in America: 'Under Orders, Under Fire,' " Programs 106 and 107 (Columbia University Seminars, presented at the Graduate School of Journalism, 16 August, 1988).

5. William L. Shirer, *Berlin Diary* (New York: A. A. Knopf, 1941), 79–80.

6. Quoted in Alex S. Jones, "Libel Suits Show Differing News Approaches of Papers, TV and Magazines," *New York Times*, 31 January 1985, p. B9.

7. Sally Bedell Smith, "Networks Pondering Budget Cuts," *New York Times*, 12 August 1985, p. C15.

8. Sally Bedell Smith, "ABC and NBC Cutting 150 News Jobs," *New York Times*, 15 October 1984, p. C17.

9. William V. Kennedy, "China's Role in a New U.S. Deterrence Strategy" (Paper presented at the U.S. Army Russian Institute, Garmisch-Partenkirchen, Germany, May 1980), published in *China, the Soviet Union, and the West*, ed. Douglas T. Stuart and William T. Tow (Boulder, Colo.: Westview, 1982), 249–61.

10. Sallie Wise, "The Soviet Domestic Impact of the War in Afghanistan" (Paper presented at the U.S. Air Force Intelligence Conference on Soviet Affairs, Arlington, Va., 19–22 October, 1988).

11. Teresa L. Waite, "As Networks Stay Home, Two Agencies Roam the World," *New York Times* 8 March 1992, p. F5.

12. William J. Small, letter to the author, 28 September 1977.

13. Quoted in "Brinkley Assails TV 'Star System' of News Reporting," *New York Times*, 16 February 1966.

14. Bill Carter, "Conservatives Call for PBS to Go Private or Go Dark," *New York Times*, 30 April 1992, p. A1.

15. Richard Bernstein, "Doubts Mar PBS Film of Black Army Unit," *New York Times*, 1 March 1993, p. B1.

16. Ibid.

17. Tony Schwartz, "The TV News, Starring Ted Turner," *New York Times*, 25 May 1980, p. F1.

18. David Marash, "20/20 Replies," *Armor* 89 (November–December 1980): 2.

19. Major General Franklin M. Davis, commandant, U.S. Army War College, conversation with author, ca. 1974.

20. Jeremy Gerard, 'Walter Cronkite: Speaking His Mind Instead of Just News," *New York Times*, 8 January 1989, p. H29.

21. Walter Goodman, 'Network News and the Push to Do Less and Do It Worse," *New York Times*, 8 February 1990, p. C22.

4

The Dailies: Shaky Bedrock

Near the end of a story "jumped" from page one on February 3, 1992, the *New York Times* reported one of the most stunning revelations of the post–Cold War era.

"After two tours in Vietnam and three years of graduate school at Yale University," the *Times* reported, "Colonel [Raoul H.] Alcala and many of his contemporaries saw the decline of the Soviet Union long before the Pentagon officially acknowledged it.

"We began to see it in 1986 and the spring of 1987," Colonel Alcala said. By this time Colonel Alcala was running a small research group for Gen. Carl E. Vuono, the Army Chief of Staff.

"Sensing the future, General Vuono mobilized his staff to formulate what he called a 'successor strategy' that would allow the Army to shrink in size, while maintaining its lethalness and mobility for any crisis."[1]

At the very time when Colonel Alcala was on duty with the U.S. mission to the North Atlantic Treaty Organization, 1979–80, this writer was assigned by a British publisher to write an assessment of the opposing NATO and Warsaw Pact land forces.[2] The format required an analysis of the opposing forces and their weapons, item by item. The results pointed overwhelmingly in one direction: The huge U.S. garrisons being maintained in Europe were superflous in light of the maturing of a West German army that could put a million trained men in the field within seventy-two hours with equipment at least equal to anything in the hands of the U.S. forces.

Evidence all the way back to World War II indicated that the Soviets could not effectively manage so complex an enterprise as a combined land and air offensive into Western Europe.[3] The single most important human element of all modern armies, navies, and air forces, and probably of all the armies of history as well, is a professional non-commissioned officer corps. The Soviet army, however, consisted of an aggregation of officers in charge of a mass of two-year conscripts without a professional non-commissioned officer corps.

In a review of that and related analyses published in *Naval War College Review*, then Assistant Deputy Secretary of Defense for Policy Dov Zakheim stated that it "may be the most valuable [assessment] ever published on the military balance."[4] What that said was that there was nothing in the government's classified files that rendered invalid anything I had garnered from open sources.

Yet in the same year that analysis was published, President Ronald Reagan and his secretary of defense, Caspar Weinberger, began a profligate military buildup. A huge part of that effort was aimed at reequipping that superfluous U.S. garrison in Europe with an even more expensive array of weapons.

So now we know that, even as that buildup was underway, the U.S. Army itself knew that it was unnecessary. Colonel Alcala plainly had drawn the same conclusions from his NATO tour that I had drawn from writing the book. But it is too much to expect any bureaucratic institution to call for reducing itself. Nor was anyone in the Office of the Secretary of Defense going to tell Weinberger or his chief that together they were squandering huge sums of the taxpayers' hard-earned cash, almost all of which was going to Republican financial supporters.

The one institution in American life that was capable of taking the case for troop withdrawal from Europe to the American public was the press. Yet the press never caught on. Oh, space was allotted here and there on an op-ed page or in other forums of individual opinion to the voices in the wilderness calling for troop withdrawal from Europe, but the reports and analyses in the news columns that could have stirred the public and moved Congress to action never appeared.

Why? Because the newspaper to which all of American journalism looks as its guide for recognition of trends the *New York Times*, had destroyed its own capability for timely and accurate analysis of complex military events. And since television news organizations are utterly dependent on the newspapers for reporting and analysis of any depth, no one would ever dare to take the lead in reporting so sharp a departure from the conventional wisdom. That failure of American journalism, in particular of the *New York Times*, cost taxpayers at least $100 billion, money spent defending affluent Europeans, all of whom enjoyed cradle-to-grave health insurance, while tens of millions of Americans had no health insurance whatever.

Checking police blotters, reviewing court records, and publishing birth and wedding announcements and obituaries comprise the routine, often lonely and thankless work of such as Phil DeVecci of the weekly *Wiscasset* (Me.) *Times*. Yet he and thousands of others like him, working on the weeklies and the small and big-city dailies bring to light most of what all the mass communications media and ultimately the public know about what is happening in our society.

There are still men and women at this bedrock level of American journalism such as Bill Britch, for half a century police reporter for the *Harrisburg* (Pa.) *Evening News*. Nearly a year spent on the western front in World War I with the 28th Infantry Division gave Britch a lifetime of empathy with the mixture of tedium and danger that makes up the life of the police officer and the professional firefighter. In his head or in a deskful of notes, Britch had at least a third of any given police or fire story written before it happened. He knew Harrisburg police officers, firefighters, and public safety officials by first name, last name, and middle initial and often their home addresses and parents as well. Much the same could be said of Al Hammond who covered local business for the *Evening News*.

That expertise was the product of assignment to a single beat, day in and day out whether anything was happening that day or not, year in and year out. In broader areas, that same sort of specialization enabled journalists such as Meyer Berger of the *New York Times* to produce feature stories that transcended their own day and passed into literature.

The quintessential beat of American journalism is sports. No one survives flubbed names and statistics in sports reporting, and there is no limit to what U.S. publishers and broadcasters will spend to assure that no sports event from the most obscure high school wrestling match to the Olympics is reported in less than infinite detail.

For a time between the end of World War I and the end of World War II it seemed that reporting and analysis of national defense would be accorded at least a fraction of the resources that go into producing the sports section of any medium-size U.S. daily. Here and there a reporter such as Mark Watson of the *Baltimore Sun*, often a veteran of either military or journalistic service in World War I, had been permitted to specialize in military reporting. In all but one instance, however, they commanded no resources other than their own salary, desk, telephone, and meagre expense account. The one exception was Hanson W. Baldwin of the *New York Times*.

The emergence of a small, but enormously significant, center for defense journalism at the *Times* was the result of a unique combination of personalities and circumstances. Thanks to a happy choice of husband by the daughter of the man who made the *New York Times* the preeminent U.S. newspaper, Arthur Hays Sulzberger became publisher of the *Times* in 1935. Already on board, and to continue as number two man (general manager), was Arthur Ochs Adler, also of the *Times*'s ruling family. Adler had served in World War I and was a major general in the Army Reserve.

Although too young to have served in World War I, Hanson W. Baldwin was a graduate of the Naval Academy, had served on active duty in the Navy and Merchant Marine, and had worked as a general assignment reporter on the *Baltimore Sun* before joining the *Times*, initially as a general assignment reporter. By 1934 Baldwin's expressed interest in the military had led to an increasing orientation to that field, so much so that the Navy attempted to make use of his continuing Reserve status to pressure him into revealing sources of a story the Navy didn't like. Baldwin responded by resigning from the Naval Reserve.[5] By that time, also, as members of a prominent Jewish family, Sulzberger and Adler had become convinced that Adolph Hitler would lead Germany into war.

"Arthur Sulzberger . . . saw . . . that there was likely to be a war in Europe, and he said he wanted me to specialize . . . on the military. . . . I got direct access to him," Baldwin recalled. That direct access—ironically what the old German general staff had called the *Immediatvortag*, the most highly prized of all staff relationships—was reflected in an equally important decision: Baldwin would remain in New York, out of the suffocating Washington routine, but close enough to the capital to get there on the morning train.

In 1937 Sulzberger sent Baldwin to "take a hard look at the armies, navies and air forces of all the principal powers in Europe." To what would be a recurring overseas travel budget of that scope was added support sufficient to enable Baldwin to "get to nearly every one of the important centers of [U.S.] tactical thought about once every two years." Never before or since has an American journalist received that sort of support for coverage of military affairs. As a result, Baldwin related, "I grew up with a lot of younger officers before they came up to high rank. That really is the only way to cover the military."

Also unique in the history of American journalism, Baldwin was eventually assigned a full-time research assistant competent to keep track of professional military publications and related sources, enabling Baldwin to travel and to develop priority stories in depth without losing touch with routine matters that could develop into tomorrow's stories. Routine defense reporting from Washington was handled by the *Times*'s Washington bureau.

The wisdom of the investment Sulzberger and Adler had made in Baldwin was demonstrated during World War II by reporting and analysis that won Baldwin a Pulitzer Prize and established the *Times* as the preeminent source of national and international military coverage. Sadly, the effect was to give virtually all the rest of American journalism an excuse for doing absolutely nothing.

Through the New York Times News Service, all other major U.S. dailies had access to Baldwin's work, and so Baldwin's strengths became the strengths of American journalism in defense reporting and analysis, and his weaknesses the weaknesses of all. Baldwin was a man of his origins and era. His ideal of the U.S. military was what he called a "homogeneous" (i.e., white Anglo-Saxon male) establishment. The idea of admitting women to the Naval Academy horrified him. He was quick to expose transgressions by the political generals of the National Guard, but very tender of the sensibilities of fellow service academy graduates, and especially of the Army

Reserve, beloved of *Times* General Manager Julius Ochs Adler whom Baldwin always referred to as "General." He knew on which side the bread was buttered.

The warp those weaknesses introduced into Baldwin's work could have been readily corrected if even one other major newspaper, most likely the *Washington Post*, had accorded defense reporting the same sort of priority it was getting on the *Times*.

With the assignment of Anthony Liviero, a World War II combat veteran and a lieutenant colonel in the Army Reserve, to Washington bureau defense coverage in the 1950s, the *Times* military coverage reached its peak, providing for at least a brief time a model of how properly organized and trained journalists could penetrate the fog of obfuscation generated by the defense bureaucracy. With the death of Liviero there began a gradual and eventually precipitous slide to disaster.

That disaster is called "Vietnam." Because it changed so fundamentally the relationship between the military and the press, and, as subsequent events would prove, between the press and the American public, it is dealt with separately in a later chapter.

The *New York Times* defense coverage has never recovered. The strongly ideological editors who gained control of the *Times*'s news operations during the Vietnam debacle have been careful to avoid creating another center for defense coverage such as that represented by Baldwin, regarding such as Baldwin and Liviero as "pro-military." Only one reporter, Richard Halloran, whose credentials as both a journalist and a military specialist are comparable to Baldwin's, has been assigned to defense coverage during the past twenty years, and Halloran says his assignment was seen by his Washington bureau colleagues as an assignment to "Siberia."[6]

Even so, Arthur Ochs Sulzberger, son and successor of Arthur Hays Sulzberger, made a feeble attempt to reconstitute *Times* defense coverage during the 1970s by hiring Marine Corps Lieutenant General Bernard Trainor upon his retirement from the service. Apparently, Sulzberger had the notion of making Trainor, in New York, the "Hanson Baldwin" to Halloran's "Liviero," in Washington. Trainor, however, could not stop acting like a general, in particular a Marine Corps general. Invited to participate in a media seminar at the Naval War College, he refused to shut up after his allotted time and went on bullying his way through the entire program, shutting out the other participants.[7] Also, whatever Sulzberger's original design, the working-level editors, still including those who had eventually stifled Hanson Baldwin, saw to it that Trainor got into print with only the most routine and innocuous stories. After one of the shortest and most dismal careers in the history of national-level journalism, Trainor disappeared into the mists of academe at Harvard's Kennedy School of Government, to be resurrected as a network "consultant" during the Persian Gulf War.

Upon Halloran's retirement from "Siberia" to a more salubrious climate in Hawaii, in January 1990, the *Times*'s military coverage went utterly adrift. In place of the leading-edge coverage with which Baldwin, Liviero, and Halloran had distinguished the paper there are routinely stories that cite as their source, five or six paragraphs down, the *Washington Post*, the *Los Angeles Times*, or one of the service-oriented publications, such as *Army Times*, but all laden with the strong ideological "slant" that had come to dominate the *Times*'s approach to news coverage during and subsequent to the Vietnam era.

What the 1990s' *Times* gets in terms of original defense reporting is almost invariably a handout from a dissident within the defense establishment who is in tune with the *Times*'s post-Vietnam, antimilitary point of view. Such was the case with the delivery, early in 1992, to Patrick E. Tyler of the *Times*'s Washington bureau of Department of Defense secret documents outlining strategic planning scenarios designed to shape the U.S. armed forces in the era following disintegration of the Soviet Union.

The question of whether the U.S. government has a right to "classify" information as secret or otherwise and the question of whether journalists have a right to determine on their own authority whether to print or broadcast such information, unlawfully acquired, are of enormous importance in themselves and will be addressed in a separate chapter.

Whatever the ramifications of those questions, the reader needed to look no further than the headline at the top of page one on February 17, 1992, to understand what the *Times* wanted the reader to think of the whole thing, even before he or she got down to what was supposedly a straight news story: "Pentagon *Imagines New Enemies* to Fight in Post-Cold-War Era: *Planning for Hypothetical Wars and Big Budgets*" (emphasis added).

Nothing but the crassest motives are imputed here. Plainly no one in the process, at least so the headline writer wanted the reader to believe, could possibly have been motivated by a genuine concern for the safety of the country in a world now far more uncertain than in the Cold War era.

"Maintaining forces capable of fighting and winning one or more of the seven [planning] scenarios outlined in the documents," the reader is instructed in paragraph two, "would require a robust level of defense spending into the next century." And it is long-standing *Times* editorial policy, clearly and forcefully reiterated almost weekly on the editorial page, that no such "robust level of defense spending" is to be tolerated.

The sources cited on page one are, successively, "internal Pentagon documents . . . classified documents." Not until the third paragraph of the continued story on page eight is the reader informed that "The 70 pages of planning documents were made available to the *New York Times* by an official who wished to call attention to what he considered vigorous attempts within the military establishment to invent a menu of alarming war scenarios that can be used by the Pentagon to prevent further reductions in forces or cancellations of new weapon systems from defense contractors."

There is no hint here or elsewhere that a law has been broken. We are left with the impression of an official with the highest possible motives, who has taken it upon himself or herself to expose the base, self-serving motives of the entire civilian and military chain of command of the Department of Defense. Nor is there any explanation of why the *New York Times* felt justified in ignoring the "classified" markings—most likely Secret or Top Secret—in deciding to publish the contents of the planning papers. Yet during the previous decade U.S. juries had seen fit to send to prison three U.S. citizens for doing essentially the same thing, two for having turned such papers over to Israel and one for having sold classified documents to his foreign employer, a British defense periodical. To whom did the public entrust responsibility for its defense? The civilian and military command of the Department of Defense, supported by the Congress and the judiciary, or the *New York Times*?

Close reading of the following twenty-four inches or so of type reveals that the planning scenarios were not "imagined," but were the product of a fairly rigorous examination of what the intelligence agencies, and the press, had been able to foresee concerning the trends in a world in which, among other things, there was even less assurance than in the past of who controlled some 23,000 nuclear weapons in the arsenal of the former Soviet Union. Any general staff that failed to identify plausible dangers on the basis of such information and to propose forces to cope with such dangers would be guilty of criminal negligence. And, indeed, all past history says that no one would be quicker than the press to condemn those same defense authorities if the "hypothetical" were to materialize as a military surprise for which the country was inadequately prepared.

The reader of what the *Times* plainly handled as an exposé is not given the luxury of testing each of the seven planning scenarios for plausibility in the light of reasonably objective analysis. The analysis was done in the headline. Believe any of these, the *Times* has told us, and you will be vulnerable to the same sort of ridicule we have directed at the planners. And if that reader still dares to attempt independent judgment, he or she is given to understand that "Some important voices... a number of analysts"—indeed, members of Congress—are likely to offer "significant challenges." But in case there are discordant voices among the members of Congress, we are warned that "For some members of Congress, the scenarios in an election year undoubtedly will provide a compelling argument to keep open defense production lines that otherwise would be slated for closing."

This is the language not of the reporter, but of the policy writer. It is carefully and deliberately crafted to assure underpinning in the news columns for judgments that the editorial board of the *New York Times* had arrived at, and published, months before based at least as much on ideology as on selective reading of the world and domestic U.S. situation.

The most demanding and potentially most dangerous of the seven planning scenarios, and the one most ridiculed in successive *Times* news coverage and editorials, portrayed an attempt by Russia, or what is now known as Belarus, to assert a territorial claim against Lithuania, with the United States coming to Lithuania's defense.

On February 24, seven days after the appearance of the *Times*'s defense scenarios story, the foreign minister of Belarus told a visiting European Community delegation that Belarus intended to assert a territorial claim against Lithuania that would include even Vilnius, the Lithuanian capital, and thereby effectively return the country to Belarus-Russian control. That report was published by the *Times* under the smallest and faintest headline type available, at the bottom of page seven, without reminding the reader that the story connected directly with one of the ridiculed planning scenarios. Yet such "connectors" are standard *Times* operating policy—in all stories, that is, in which the connection would not undercut a previously established editorial page position.

If this is the status of defense reporting in the world's premiere newspaper, what of the runners-up?

Throughout the Persian Gulf War and thereafter, the *Wall Street Journal* stumbled into, around, and out of the central story of the war—the spectacular performances of the U.S. and French air cavalry on the western flank—without at any point recognizing its import. Indeed, so fixated did the *Journal*'s Pentagon and principal war correspondent get with the trees that he never really did get out of the forest. In a book published a year after the war, he was still obsessed with such peripheral problems as the restrictions of the military press control system, still unaware that the most important story of all had been on the public record all along. Lacking such perception, the *Journal* fell innocently and completely in with the Army's bold defense of its force structure status quo.

On April 19, 1992, John Fialka, covering the Pentagon for the *Journal*, published an elaborate report comparing the AH–64 attack helicopter, heart of the Army's air cavalry, with the fixed-wing Air Force A–10, designed and produced too late to cope with the sort of intense automatic weapons anti-aircraft fire encountered in Vietnam.

Fialka missed a central point: The AH–64 in company with the scout and troop-carrying helicopters with which it was designed to operate could seize and hold terrain and, indeed, had done just that with spectacular results a few months before in the Gulf War. The A–10 could do no such thing. But by narrowing the comparison to the very limited roles performed by the A–10, Fialka led himself into the trap of touting an aircraft that the Air Force was seeking to discard as being designed to too narrow a focus. The Army, however, responded with glee. By taking up the cudgels on the very limited grounds Fialka had so conveniently marked off, it was able to have the best of all worlds: appearing to loyally defend its air cavalry forces, while at the same time disguising the overwhelming evidence that its paratrooper and heavy armored forces were now about as useful as the chariot and the horse cavalry.

The enormity of the strategic and economic implications of this technological change in land warfare, demonstrated workable in the Gulf War, and of the failure of American journalism to recognize its implications, even with all of the facts spread out before it, simply cannot be overemphasized.

Fialka was not the cause of the *Journal*'s problem: he was its victim. *Journal* reporters come and go at the Pentagon, the place being plainly regarded by that newspaper and its staff exactly as do the editors and staff of the *New York Times*, as a "Siberia" to be gotten away from as quickly as possible. Like his predecessors, Fialka never was given the time or the training to cope with the complexities of the job.

Short of war, no more than fifteen national press representatives are assigned to cover the "Pentagon" (i.e., U.S. defense worldwide). Among the tiny groups of newspapers represented the most curious arrangement is that of the *Washington Post*. The *Post* had a defense reporter, John G. Norris, who was a contemporary of the *Times*'s Hanson Baldwin, but Norris never had more than a tiny fraction of the editorial prestige and financial support given Baldwin and none of Baldwin's direct access to the owners. That meant that he truly covered only "the Pentagon"—the Washington policy end of defense—in a role and at a level of responsibility more analogous to that of the *Times*'s Anthony Liviero rather than to that of Baldwin in New York.

Norris was replaced by George C. Wilson, a World War II Navy veteran, who, if anything, was kept even more remote from top management, so remote that he was permitted to go off for seven months of an aircraft carrier without apparently being much missed. The inside track in *Washington Post* defense reporting was given to people closer to the throne who were being groomed for better things. Their most distinguishing common trait has been that they began the Pentagon assignment innocent of any prior contact with or instruction about the military whatsoever and received as little as possible thereafter.

Typical among these was Fred Hiatt, and just as typical of what they achieved, or did not achieve, was Hiatt's swan song, written after three years as defense reporter when he was reassigned to cover Japan, a subject for which he was at least equally untrained. "As an upper-middle-class Harvard-bound high school senior in 1972," Hiatt wrote, "I never considered volunteering [for Vietnam service]. . . . My first day on the [Pentagon] beat, I would have been hard put to tell a colonel from a corporal."[8]

What other profession at the end of the twentieth century would give a practitioner that level of responsibility at a comparable level of competence? An attorney or a surgeon so ignorant of even the basic terminology of his or her day-to-day work would not be admitted to the bar or permitted to practice as a member of a hospital staff. Yet, at a time when the United States could have been destroyed in half an hour by a then still functioning Soviet Union, Hiatt was assigned to sort out for his readers the enormous complexities involved in that military relationship.

"My ventures to Army bases in Germany," Hiatt wrote at the end of his three-year Pentagon assignment, "fighter-pilot schools in Nevada and cruisers and carriers in the Atlantic have provided the basic training I escaped as a young adult."[9] That is an astonishing, and a damning, statement. That Hiatt would have taken off to Tokyo with him the notion that the carefully orchestrated, red-carpet, very-important-person, high-level officer treatment he received on those "ventures" made up for the "basic training" he chose to avoid is even more frightening than his confession of military illiteracy at the beginning of his defense assignment.

There were no wet clothes on those "ventures," certainly not for days at a time. There were no missed meals and no days without convivial happy-hour talk in a warm, dry wardroom or at the bar of an officers' club. There were no blistered heels and none of the lonely, miserable days and sleepless nights that begin to introduce the most ordinary peacetime enlisted basic trainee to the realities of war. So what the *Washington Post* had produced by sending Hiatt to the Pentagon was a newly minted member of that part of American society that lives in a world over and above the lot of the vast majority of the country's population, but that determines by the quality or lack thereof of the information it provides who among that vastly larger population will serve or not serve, live or die in time of war, and that has effectively insulated itself from such hazards in anything short of all-out nuclear war.

What Hiatt claimed to have learned from his short tenure on the military beat was that "the troops are better than I thought and the Brass far worse."[10]

The prospect of assignment to the Pentagon is almost universally loathed among those U.S. military officers who truly gain their greatest satisfaction from unit-level military operations and training. Long before Hiatt had finally found out the difference between a corporal and a colonel those majors and lieutenant commanders, not much older by and large than Hiatt when he began his Pentagon tour, had come to believe that not only the Pentagon, but also Washington—not excluding Washington journalism—is a jungle of lies and obfuscation in which people of uncompromising integrity are unlikely to survive. They have long had a little joke that Hiatt might have come across if his "ventures" had been preceded by a few years spent covering a more distant military command. "Cover off and stand tall," the little ditty ends, "as you enter the gates of Hell, for your arrival will be observed by the general staffs of all the nations on earth."

Any officer who has served on a battalion staff has met the equivalent of Major Jimmy Sinclair, the dedicated careerist and svelt service politician in that classic film study of command *Tunes of Glory*, starring Alec Guinness and John Mills. And any officer who has served on a division or higher staff has met the penultimately corrupt general staff officer portrayed by Adolphe Menjou in the equally classic film *Paths of Glory*.

But what Hiatt plainly never understood, even as he wrote his bitter farewell to his Pentagon tour, is that military politicians such as Jimmy Sinclair and cruelly cynical officers such as that played by Adolphe Menjou are able to perform at their worst in the Pentagon and get away with it at the expense of people of integrity because the *Washington Post* assigns innocents such as Fred Hiatt to cover them.

How much can be gotten past a Washington press establishment that depends on such as Hiatt for defense coverage was apparent in an event that occurred while he was still on the Pentagon beat and just four months before publication of his "Parting Shot."

When the U.S. government decided, early in 1986, that it should attempt to kill Colonel Muammar Qaddafi or at least cripple his outlaw regime in Libya, it had at its disposal three aircraft carriers in the Atlantic and the Mediterranean and all the time necessary to form them into a task force that could have provided all of the firepower needed. At least as important, those ships would have had all of the electronic countermeasures necessary to assure that the Libyan air defense could neither acquire early warning of the approach of the attacking U.S. aircraft nor acquire the data needed to control anti-aircraft missiles.

But, as it turned out, only two aircraft carriers were assigned to the mission, flown on April 14. In place of the missing carrier, U.S. Air Force F–111 fighter-bombers based in Britain had been used. One of those F–111s was lost with its two-man crew.

Stansfield Turner, a former director of the Central Intelligence Agency (CIA), and a few Washington reporters, Hiatt of the *Post* among them, sensed that something was wrong. Most of the doubters thought, as did the former CIA director,[11] that the peculiar arrangement had been designed to give the Air Force "a piece of the action." Hiatt found "analysts inside and outside the military" were raising a tantalizing question as to whether the F–111s were inserted into the raid because of some special need to dramatize then British Prime Minister Margaret Thatcher's support for her U.S. ally. But he failed to follow up on his discovery.[12]

Drawing on his intimate knowledge of carrier operations and extensive contacts in the Navy, George Wilson of the *Post* was able to establish that the Navy had carried out its part of the mission to perfection—all targets attacked successfully, all aircraft returned safely—and that the Navy A–6s used were every bit as capable as the F–111s. Peter Grier of the *Christian Science Monitor* likewise found sources who affirmed that there was no military reason for including the F–111s.

Halloran of the *Times*, a former paratrooper, had no background in long-range flight operations, but he had a gut feeling about what is right and wrong in military operations in general. In no small part because of his military background, he had the trust of military officers who were concerned enough themselves about the peculiar aspects of the Libya raid to seek him out. " 'Do you really think,' an Air Force officer asked Halloran of the 14-hour F–111 flights, far beyond anything the aircraft had been designed to perform, in particular as concerns human endurance, 'that any military officer would have asked a pilot to fly all that way? I think those planners should be unstrapped from their desks and strapped into those cockpits.' "[13]

Time would report that the surviving F–111 crews were so cramped by the time they got back to their home bases that cranes had to be used to lift some of them out of their cockpits.[14] *Armed Forces Journal International* noted that the only bombs available for the F–111s were "antique."[15] In an article unrelated to the Libya mission *Air Force* magazine described the F–111 as a "maintenance nightmare."

Picking up from the Halloran coverage, Judith Miller, Middle East correspondent for the *Times*, found that Maltese air controllers had given Libya thirty to forty-five minutes warning of the incoming F–111s, plenty of time to alert air defense missile batteries and to acquire firing data.[16] The Navy, attacking from just over the horizon and with a plenitude of electronic countermeasures to support at least its own strike aircraft, accorded the Libyans no such luxuries.

What did not make military sense began to make political sense. Immediately after the raid an extradition treaty aimed at Irish Republican Army guerrillas who had sought asylum in the United States that had been languishing in the U.S. Senate for months prior to the Libya raid with scant likelihood of passage was revived and shortly thereafter ratified by the Senate. Upon their departure from office the president and the secretary of defense who had sent that F–111 crew to a needless death and subjected all the others to torment and equivalent unnecessary risks were awarded British knighthoods.

In 1992 a principal target of the extradition treaty, Joseph P. Doherty, was returned to British control, albeit under different legal auspices. At that time Michael Sullivan, London correspondent of National Public Radio,[17] and others quoted British sources that acknowledged a direct connection between the extradition treaty and Doherty's subsequent return and the use of the F–111s in the Libya raid to generate senatorial support for British policy.

Alert, aggressive pursuit of all the evidence lying about would not have saved the lives of the two F–111 crewmen, but it would almost certainly have blocked the knighthoods—a repudiation of the spirit, if not the letter, of the U.S. Constitution—and thus dissuaded future policy-makers from playing political games with American lives. Official Washington will continue to get away with such outrages so long as it knows that the journalistic dislike of the military will continue to assure coverage of the Pentagon by people ill-equipped to deal with the subterfuges and the nuances of the defense story.

At the *Washington Post*, Fred Hiatt was replaced by Molly Moore, another reporter equally innocent of the distinction "between a colonel and a corporal." George Wilson remained until retirement in the *Washington Post*'s version of "Siberia." How much this peculiar arrangement on the *Post* reflects a deep ideological orientation throughout the *Post*'s hierarchy was revealed by Meg Greenfield, editorial page editor of the *Post*, in a commentary published on April 25, 1984. "I have just come back from a couple of days . . . in fabled Dr. Strangeloveland," Greenfield wrote. "I spent one day at Offutt Air Force Base near Omaha, site of the Strategic Air Command (SAC) [Headquarters], and one day at Whiteman Air Force Base in Missouri, home of . . . 150 Minuteman II nuclear-armed missiles."[18]

"Strangeloveland." Yet a long stretch of type later, Greenfield would allow that none of the people she met in those two days quite resembled the mad characters of the film, but first she had to deal with a more pressing problem. "Since I and my colleagues have been writing copiously [about SAC] over the years, it did not seem amiss to me to wish to have a look."

The reader who might have thought journalists "have a look" before "writing copiously" should note that the *Washington Post* has a different approach.

"I mention this [desire to have a look] somewhat defensively because [of] the attitude that greets a returning visitor from bombsville.

"It ranges from mild surprise through perplexity and incredulity to sheer astonishment; why did you go? The question, put by different friends and colleagues, always seemed to bear a note of anxiety. Perhaps, as in some ancient superstition, there was a sense that by going to the place where the planes and missiles would be launched, I risked having something lethal brush off on me, or being deformed by what I had beheld. . . .

"What all this said to me was that revulsion, fright and taboo . . . had prompted a kind of ostrichlike attitude in otherwise sophisticated people. They think it better to live with fantasies. . . . "

Greenfield's "friends and colleagues" were the top editors of the *Washington Post*. No wonder George Wilson and his ilk have been kept in "Siberia" all these years or that a succession of military illiterates has been assigned to the inside track of *Post* Pentagon coverage. Only by such a policy could the ostriches protect their "fantasies."

Not least among those fantasies is the notion that nothing important happens outside of Washington, D.C., at least with respect to the making of U.S. government policy.

When, in January 1980, President Jimmy Carter proclaimed his intention to defend the Persian Gulf from a Soviet Union then threatening in Afghanistan, Carter's hand-picked Army chief of staff, Edward C. Meyer, and the Army's deputy chief of staff for operations, then Lieutenant General

Glenn K. Otis, got then Major General Jack Merritt, commandant of the Army War College at Carlisle Barracks, Pennsylvania, to cook up one of the phoniest "studies" ever inflicted on the long-victimized taxpayer. Merritt was handed a list of five U.S. Army divisions until then deemed to be on shaky budgetary ground and was told to "prove" that they could be gotten to the Middle East in time to prevent twenty-seven Soviet motorized infantry and tank divisions, plus seven airborne divisions with the largest fleet of troop-carrying helicopters in the world available to move them, all backed by fleets of bombers, salvoes of long-range missiles, and the largest submarine fleet in the world, from taking over the Persian Gulf oil fields.

The principal vehicle for the "study" would be an electronic war game.[19] Because none of the circuits could be secured, the war game had to be played out entirely in the unclassified mode. Merritt staffed the "study" (Parametric Force Analysis), and the war game, largely with military neophytes and illiterates. Among them was a civilian economist who was to function as the commander of Soviet air forces in southern Asia. His introduction to his new duties began with "North is at the top of the map, west is at the left."

So that all concerned would not miss the point, Merritt made it plain in his opening remarks to the study team that his promotion to lieutenant general depended on their achievement of a satisfactory result. And, sure enough, the study "proved" that the five divisions, starting from the continental United States, 12,000 miles away, could stop a Soviet juggernaut that would start from points a few hundred miles away. On the basis of that phony document the budgetary future of the five divisions was secured.

The junior editors of the *Washington Post*'s Sunday "Outlook" accepted an article from the author describing the scam and were preparing to run the article under the imaginative headline "The War Game We Played on Ourselves." When the project came to the attention of the senior editor, Robert Kaiser, however, it was squelched.

Kaiser simply refused to believe that U.S. national defense policy is made anywhere outside of Washington or by any process except thorough, objective analysis.[20] At that moment a Marine Corps lieutenant colonel was conducting an outlaw war from the basement of the White House annex that would shake the U.S. government to its sandals. The *Washington Post* and, indeed, all of the major newspapers represented in Washington knew something about that long before Iran-Contra finally got into the news. But all were victims of their inability to believe that a lowly lieutenant colonel could be playing such an important role, and right under their noses.

And that, in turn, is a product of their studied refusal to recognize the military as worthy of intense, specialized coverage, starting with some form of active military service. Had Kaiser run the story about the phony Army War College study and had the *Post*'s news editors followed it up, they would not have missed the nuclear implications of the U.S. decision to intervene in the Persian Gulf in 1990.

Meyer, Otis, and Merritt could not have gotten away with the fraudulent Parametric Force Analysis study if Generals George C. Marshall and Dwight D. Eisenhower had been successful in their efforts at the end of World War II to do away with the service war colleges in favor of a single National War College in which self-serving efforts to bolster the budget of a single service would be under the scrutiny of at least the other services. The defeat of the Marshall-Eisenhower initiative, largely due to opposition by the Navy, has meant that, half a century later, each service is able to "justify' its own force structure and budget using "studies" such as the one that Meyer had ordered. In the decade since the Parametric Force Analysis study was played out on jerry-rigged circuits each of the service war colleges has built an elaborate electronic war gaming establishment in secure facilities costing in the aggregate well over $100 million. Yet the end result of the "studies" supported thereby is no more credible than was that of the outrageous Parametric Force Analysis study because of the manner in which they are skewed by the highly selective assumptions from which they start.

So, had Kaiser and the other *Washington Post* editors possessed the training and background necessary to understand the implications of the phony War College study, and had Congress been forced by publication of that story to deal with the underlying problems, it is very likely that the services would not have gotten away with plunging $10 million, let alone $100 million, into the redundant war gaming systems. It is at least as likely that we would now have the single, more honest senior service college that Marshall and Eisenhower tried to create.

With the retirement of Richard Halloran in 1990 the *New York Times* came to rely more and more on the *Los Angeles Times* as well as the *Washington Post* for defense coverage other than such handouts, legal or otherwise, as in the "seven scenarios" story. The *Los Angeles Times* covers the Pentagon by such as Melissa Healy, a journalistic twin of the *Washington Post's* Fred Hiatt in terms of lack of military background, but with at least some Washington defense reporting experience before she joined the *Times*. And the concentration of defense industries in its market area has forced the *Los Angeles Times* to develop a narrowly focused expertise on those industries. There is no coordinated management of these capabilities, however, leaving vast gaps of comprehension and reporting between and among them.

The *Los Angeles Times* makes no more sustained effort to cover the military outside of Washington than does the *Washington Post*. On the rare occasions when a *Los Angeles Times* reporter is sent on what Hiatt of the *Post* called "ventures" the mindset of Washington journalism, so vividly, if inadvertently, described by Meg Greenfield in her revealing "Strangeloveland" commentary, goes right along—and comes back with them.

In February 1992 the Los Angeles Times News Service distributed a story by Melissa Healy in which the opening paragraphs made it appear that she had been visiting an air defense fighter base in Alaska. Whether she had, in fact, been off to Alaska became open to doubt when, in the third paragraph, it developed that the "hook"—that is, the news event that would give the story timeliness—was not goings-on in Alaska that might have been mined from an Air Force press release, but a collision a few days previous between a U.S. nuclear attack submarine, the U.S.S. *Baton Rouge*, patrolling off the Kola Inlet in northern Russia and a Russian submarine patrolling at a lower depth that had picked a most unfortunate time and place to surface. Even the reader whose acquaintance with submarines is derived from Tom Clancy novels might have begun to wonder about the marvels of technology described therein. Not so the Pentagon correspondent of the *Los Angeles Times*. Healy had different fish to fry.

The thrust of the opening paragraphs was that the fighter pilots up in Alaska could not get out of their old Cold War habit of intercepting former Soviet reconnaissance aircraft that intruded into U.S. air space. "For the crew members of the *Baton Rouge*, old habits die hard, too," Healy wrote, developing her theme. "In mid-February, the *Baton Rouge* decided in the course of a routine mission to take the game to the other team's back yard."[21]

Now there was one of the most stunning military stories of our times. At least as reported by Healy, it appears that the captain, or perhaps the crew members by a democratic process new to the Navy, had decided on some sort of whim to depart from an assigned patrol area and to take a powerful U.S. warship on an unauthorized lark into an area where it might not only collide with one of its opposite numbers, but also create an international incident of even greater proportions than that which, in fact, occurred.

If such was the case, it plainly did not occur to Healy that the captain, or whatever commune was in control of the *Baton Rouge*, might be facing a court martial over much more serious matters than the Russian submarine's bent periscope and dignity. Healy was too busy getting on to the core of her story: "More than two years after the Berlin Wall was breached and two months after the Soviet Union dissolved, many of the military activities spawned by four decades of Cold War remain essentially unchanged, proceeding almost as if on autopilot."[22]

In one form or another that story has been written so often over the past thirty years that it deserves to be enshrined as "The Story" of U.S. national defense. The stupid, inflexible "military mind" plunges on—indeed, "on autopilot"—toward war, or at the very least toward the squandering of the nation's wealth. So predictable is the pattern that the long-time reader of such stories knows before the eye gets there that, a paragraph or two later, someone from the Brookings Institution will be on hand to affirm that what the writer has been saying for the past several paragraphs is, indeed, true. Never is the reader informed that the Brookings Institution exists to sustain out-of-office Democratic political appointees and staff members until brighter days come along. They always, always argue for reduction of the defense budget and transfer of the proceeds to favored social programs, no matter what is going on in the rest of the world at the moment or how dismal the results of the last "Great Society."

Sure enough, the Brookings people are there to voice support for Healy's theme.

Healy and her soulmates at Brookings have every right to express their opinions, but not in the news columns under the guise of reporting. It would have strained the term even to call it "news analysis," but the Los Angeles Times News Service did not identify it as such. The Healy story was the out-and-out opinion of a messianic "advocacy journalist," born and bred of deep anti-military feelings during Vietnam-era college days. But so deeply is that opinion—"fantasies," to use Greenfield's term—engrained as fact in the *Los Angeles Times* Washington bureau that Healy was not required to support her amazing statement about the wanderings-on-whim of the *Baton Rouge*. If, in fact, she was wrong about that, and if the captain of that submarine was sailing exactly where the headquarters that sent him on his way had told him to go, absent any advice from the crew, then Healy plainly had no business anywhere near the national defense story.

The saddest story in terms of coverage of the military at the national and international levels has been that of the *Christian Science Monitor*. Once a truly international newspaper with a high reputation for coverage in all fields, including the military, the *Monitor* became the victim in the late 1980s of an incredibly misguided decision by its sponsoring church to divert tens of millions of dollars once available to subsidize the never-profitable newspaper into the pursuit of a radio and television audience already surfeited with choices. Unable to develop programs of sufficient quality or, more accurately, of sufficient entertainment value to carve out a niche, the Christian Science church, and the *Monitor* with it, blundered into a financial disaster.

In protest over the church's shift to the broadcast media, the editor in chief and approximately half of the *Monitor*'s formerly superior staff resigned. What remained of the paper resembled a once superb athlete who continued to look the same, except that he had lost an arm and a leg.

There are no other truly national U.S. newspapers than these. Although of high quality in regard to many of the political, economic, and social stories it does cover, the *Philadelphia Inquirer* does not bother to assign anyone full-time even to the Pentagon. The *Baltimore Sun* has assigned a full-time reporter to the Pentagon for many years, but its pro-military stance, almost unique in American journalism, is so pronounced that it has never carried much weight save as an "explainer"[23] of Pentagon policy.

This, then, is the primary basis for the television and radio broadcasts on which most of the American public has come to rely for news about national defense. The blind are leading the blind.

NOTES

1. "Plans for Small Wars Replace Fear of Big One," *New York Times*, 3 February 1992, p. A8.

2. William V. Kennedy, "Land Forces," *The Balance of Military Power: NATO and the Warsaw Pact* (London: Salamander; New York: St. Martin's, 1981).

3. To a large extent, this view reflected that of Major General Lothar Renner, German Army (Ret.), a veteran of extensive service at corps level and above on the Eastern Front during World War II. He was interviewed at Heidelberg in preparation for the book cited in note 2. General Renner's assessment tallied with the views of Eastern Front German veterans who were classmates of the author at the Armor School, Fort Knox, Kentucky, in 1956. In an interview with John G. Roos, published in the February 1993 issue of *Armed Forces Journal International* (p. 46), General Klaus Nauman, Chief of Staff of the German Armed Forces, stated, "Warsaw Pact forces might have been good in the initial controlled stages of a thrust, but after the first blood I doubt very much if they would have remained an effective force."

4. Dov S. Zakheim, book review, *The Balance of Military Power: NATO and the Warsaw Pact*, *U.S. Naval War College Review*, May-June 1982, p. 95.

5. This incident and the subsequent description of Baldwin's early career at the *Times* are taken from "Reminiscences of Hanson Weightman Baldwin," U.S. Naval Institute Oral History Program, Annapolis, Maryland, vols. I and II, 1975.

6. Richard Halloran, correspondence with the author, 3 September 1991.

7. "Darts and Laurels," *Armed Forces Journal International* (April 1990): 80.

8. Fred Hiatt, "A Parting Shot," (Outlook), *Washington Post*, 17 August 1986, p. 1.

9. Ibid.

10. Ibid.

11. Stansfield Turner, 'Military Logrolling," (Opinion) *Christian Science Monitor*, 27 June 1986. See also "Schlesinger: Use of Jets from Britain Political," *Philadelphia Inquirer*, 13 May 1986, p. 11A.

12. Fred Hiatt, "Use of Air Force Planes Raises Questions," *Washington Post*, 20 April 1986, p. A24.

13. Richard Halloran, "Hyperbole and Grins," *New York Times*, 18 April 1986, p. A16.

14. William R. Doerner, et al., "In the Dead of the Night," *Time*, 28 April 1986, p. 31.

15. "Darts and Laurels," *Armed Forces Journal International*, May 1986, p. 77.

16. Judith Miller, "Malta Says Libya Got a Tip on Raid," *New York Times*, 6 August 1986, p. 1.

17. "Morning Edition," National Public Radio, 20 February 1992.

18. Meg Greenfield, "The Keepers of the Bomb," *Washington Post*, 25 April 1984, Op Ed.

19. The writer was a participant until he was relieved for refusal to stop telling visiting generals that the Soviets already controlled most of the air space over Iran from bases within the Soviet Union and could occupy the Iranian ports and airfields within a matter of hours by employment of seven Airborne divisions from Soviet-occupied bases in Afghanistan. Two years later, the author found the Naval War

College using the same electronic war game. When asked how they were managing to deliver the huge amount of materiel required over the 12,000-mile sea line of communications, the operators said they assumed zero losses of shipping from submarines or long-range missiles and bombers. There were then some 300 submarines active in the Soviet fleet. During the last one thousand miles of their voyage the U.S. shipping would have been within the range of several hundred late model long-range bombers. That convenient assumption of zero losses underpinned several major Navy and Marine Corps budgetary accounts.

20. Robert G. Kaiser, correspondence with the author, 25 February 1983.

21. Melissa Healy, "Old (Cold War) Habits Die Hard," *Portland* (Me.) *Press Herald*, 26 February 1992, p. 2A.

22. Ibid.

23. During the many years that he appeared on Public Television's "Washington Week in Review," the *Sun*'s Pentagon correspondent, Charles Cordrry, was routinely called upon by the moderator to "explain" Pentagon policy as concerns current news stories. Neither Mr. Cordrry, nor apparently his chiefs at the *Sun*, ever objected to the role of "explainer," a role that traditional journalistic practice would assign to the Pentagon's publicists.

5

The Wire Services: The Weakest Reed

Early in 1964 reports began to appear in professional military periodicals that a major exercise was to be conducted in May. It would test for the first time the plausibility of rules governing the use of nuclear weapons in the defense of Western Europe. From stitching together these snippets of information, it became apparent that this was to be the first war gaming on anything like a realistic scale of a nuclear conflict between the forces of the North Atlantic Treaty Organization and the forces of what was then the Warsaw Pact, constituting the Soviet Union and the Eastern European nations it had incorporated into its empire through conquest in World War II.

To this day, Joint Exercise Desert Strike, conducted during the last two weeks in May of 1964 across 100,000 square miles of the Mojave Desert, is the only major military exercise ever to have put to a realistic test the pressures that could force one side or the other in such a conflict to resort to "tactical" (i.e., battlefield-size) nuclear weapons equivalent to 1,000 to 15,000 tons of TNT (1–15 kilotons). The issues raised in that test would have a frightening relevance to the opening weeks of the Persian Gulf War, in 1990–91, and a continuing validity as nuclear weapons technology spreads to an increasing array of nations, many of them unstable or under criminal leadership.

None of the reporters who routinely cover the Pentagon reported the upcoming exercise. But informed by other means of its importance, Richard Leonard, managing editor of one of the most respected major newspapers in the United States, the *Milwaukee Journal*, responded, "No question about its importance, but we'll rely on the wire services."[1]

He was referring to the Associated Press, United Press International, and

Reuters. The Associated Press (AP) is far and away the most important of the three.

"Around an office table at *The Sun* in May, 1848, ten men representing six New York City newspapers reached a historic decision," the official history of the AP relates. "The newly invented telegraph made transmission of news possible by wire but at costs so high that the resources of any single paper would be strained. . . . Thus was founded the first non-profit cooperative news organization. They called it The Associated Press."[2]

Today, some 5,000 U.S. newspapers and television and radio stations are subscribers, and there are subscribers in over one hundred foreign countries. The organization developed to serve those subscribers has not changed in any substantial way since 1848. That is, a system of bureaus was established in Washington, at regional centers throughout the United States located in the main state capitals, and in foreign capitals. With the exception of the sports reporters, a lone specialist in religion, and a handful of specialists in other fields, mainly business, the worldwide system of bureaus is staffed exclusively by general assignment reporters, primarily people educated in the liberal arts or political "science."

The entire national defense system of the United States is covered by never more than two members of a Washington bureau totaling well over one hundred, about the same level of resources devoted to the theater and television. There is no full-time coverage of any foreign national or regional military establishment. Throughout the Cold War, the worldwide military operations of the Soviet Union were covered in fragments of whoever happened to be available in the local and regional bureaus. The AP has no established system for training even the one or two Pentagon reporters assigned to full-time coverage of U.S. national defense.

As to where continuing defense coverage stands in the priorities of the AP's top management, a *New York Times* reporter was told at the height of the Cold War that the priorities were "life styles, inflation, consumerism and the environment."[3] There was one other priority, of course, so unique and so timeless in terms of its dominance over all others that it was not necessary even to mention it—sports.

Such priorities are determined on the basis of logs the wire services keep on how many newspapers use a particular story. The low priority accorded routine defense coverage reflects, therefore, the priorities of American journalism, not just those of the management of the AP.

Notoriously parsimonious, the AP has relied heavily from its start on "stringers," local correspondents generally employed by a local newspaper or broadcast station who sell their products to the AP on a piece basis. Overseas, not only the "stringers," but the full-time bureau members as well tend to be foreign nationals, a trend that has been steadily escalating as the cost of maintaining U.S. correspondents overseas has climbed. The assignment of one such foreign national, Peter Arnett, to cover crucial aspects of U.S. diplomatic and military operations became a major point of controversy during the Vietnam War and raises continuing questions in regard to the security of U.S. forces in time of war.

"The AP . . . is wholly independent and operates without subsidy, interference or influence by any government,"[4] the AP claims in its standard publications. Yet its overseas foreign employees are subject to the laws of a wide range of governments, with security laws ranging from subtle to draconian. In Britain, for example, all British citizens are subject to the Official Secrets Act by which any British civil servant can sequester information on grounds of "national security," with severe penalties imposed on any journalist who violates that diktat. Unless its British employees see their future entirely within the AP and sooner rather than later as U.S. citizens, the AP's claim to be operating "without . . . interference or influence by any government" simply cannot be supported with respect to Britain or any of the present British Commonwealth nations and former British colonies where the Official Secrets Act or derivatives thereof are in force. In much of Africa, Latin America, and Asia the penalty for violation of the local "official secrets act" is death. Thus, much of what the American and world public receive from the AP is distorted by reasonable fears on the part of its foreign staff for the consequences of looking too deeply into the affairs of their own governments.

Similar distortions occur within the wholly American staffs to the degree that those staffs must depend on local stringers. The stringer must go on living in his or her home community after whatever brief burst of journalistic glory may be derived from a story sold to the AP. It would be a very brave and perhaps foolhardy AP stringer who would file a story that might lead to the closing or downsizing of a local military installation or defense-related industry employing hundreds or thousands of friends, family members, and neighbors.

From the language of its own promotional literature, it is apparent that, to the management of the AP, capital investment is understood to be expenditures for improved transmission facilities for both words and pictures. The AP has never made a major comparable investment in the training of personnel. That has always been the responsibility of the employee.

Even so, in 1977 two AP writers, Arnett and Fred S. Hoffman, given two months and the means to travel to U.S. military headquarters worldwide, were able to establish that there were serious deficiencies in all major military categories. Arnett by that time had gained extensive experience with military affairs in Vietnam, and Hoffman had spent many years as the AP's principal, often sole, Pentagon correspondent. The series they wrote was an important influence in persuading President Jimmy Carter to raise defense spending during the latter part of his administration. In both cases, that expertise was the product of accident, rather than design.

More common to AP coverage of defense is the observation by former

Assistant Secretary of Defense for Public Affairs Phil Goulding: "When a major Pentagon announcement is read in the reporters' room, the [AP] may attempt to get a head start by having one man listen and take notes while the other simultaneously dictates on the telephone to a rewrite man in his main office in Washington. This breeds inaccuracy. . . ."[5] It also breeds a situation wherein the only two people in the entire AP who are paid to think about national defense cannot think beyond the next Pentagon handout.

Thirteen years before the Arnett-Hoffman series, on the eve of Joint Exercise Desert Strike, Hoffman was much greener at the Pentagon job. He was so green, in fact, that he did not catch the significance of the notices hinting at a landmark nuclear exercise. Typical of his fellow editors throughout the country, the *Milwaukee Journal*'s managing editor, Richard Leonard, paid so little attention to how the AP goes about covering national defense that he was unaware that, except for its journeyman Pentagon reporter, the AP had no one who was capable of recognizing the importance of the exercise, or of covering it.

That the AP simply was not competent to cover something so complex as Desert Strike became apparent very quickly in the opening seventy-two hours of the exercise.[6]

Land forces simulating those of NATO and the Warsaw Pact were deployed on opposite sides of the Colorado River. They were supported by Air Force units assembled from all over the United States, operating from base throughout the western third of the country. The distances involved, the totality of territory covered, and the reasonably representational land forces, the largest concentration of modern armored forces ever assembled in North America, gave the exercise a scale and a validity impossible to duplicate except in war—and probably impossible to duplicate as a major maneuver today.

At least as significant as the forces themselves were the opposing "governments" made up of ambassadorial-level Foreign Service officers and retired military officers. All had direct experience with the rules governing the release of nuclear weapons under NATO and all had access to the intelligence concerning the granting of such authority under the opposing Warsaw Pact.

The opening three days of the exercise were devoted mainly to reconnaissance. Because of the sensitivity of anything dealing with nuclear weapons, the State Department did everything it possibly could to obscure and play down the meaning of the exercise. That accounted for the paucity of early notice. The exercise director, however, Army General Paul D. Adams, believed that the members of the public, whose lives were at stake, en masse, should know everything possible about the exercise if they were to be able to make intelligent policy choices. Had the press, including the AP correspondents sent out from Los Angeles, understood the crucial nature of the early reconnaissance activities, they would have asked to accompany the air observers and armored cavalry units involved, and Adams was prepared to grant any such request.

No one was the least interested in the reconnaissance activities. Nor were they much interested in the elaborate control system by which both human and equipment casualties would be assessed, a crucial consideration if anyone had been inclined to believe the military was simply going to act out a prearranged scenario. The three days of on-the-scene AP coverage were wasted on "color" stories, ranging from a general who stepped on a rattlesnake to the reaction of such local townsfolk as could be located and interviewed in the widely scattered desert communities.

The AP correspondents and most of the rest had given up on finding anything exciting and were back in their beds in Los Angeles when the opposing "Warsaw Pact" forces launched an attack that very quickly began to roll up the defending "NATO" flank. Going precisely by the NATO rules, the defending commander waited until he had a convincing case for authority to use nuclear weapons, the last "reserve" available to him.

The NATO "government" went through all of the established procedures and granted the requested authority six hours later, a remarkably short time considering the need for communications, assemblage of the required national leaders and so on. That was six hours too late. By then, defending and opposing units were hopelessly intermixed. It would have been impossible to locate and engage a target without running an unacceptable risk that the ground would be occupied by a friendly unit by the time the weapon exploded. The lesson of Desert Strike was and remains stark in its simplicity: When a commander can prove that he or she must resort to nuclear firepower, that is the moment when he or she must start using it. Any delay, certainly any delay such as required by the elaborate NATO rules, would be fatal.

Whether one agreed with that lesson or not, some $57 million of hard-earned taxpayer 1964 dollars had been spent to develop it. A presidential campaign was underway in which the degree of control over nuclear weapons—in particular the question of whether the U.S. supreme allied commander in Europe should be delegated authority in advance to use such weapons—would become a major issue. None of the expensive Desert Strike information ever reached the general public, chiefly because the AP was unable to comprehend its significance.

Nothing could persuade the Los Angeles AP correspondents to return to the hot, dusty, thoroughly confusing exercise area. So General Adams had his twice-daily communiques flown to Los Angeles and carried to the AP office. Those communiques spelled out, hour by hour, the progress of the exercise, including all of the nuclear information. Nothing was held back. If a staff officer would not release information, an appeal would be made to General Adams, and, invariably, he directed that the information be released.

If all of that constituted a giant military fraud intended to support delegation of authority to the supreme commander in Europe, that certainly was an important national story in itself. But lacking the technical competence to make a judgment about the information one way or another, the AP chose to say nothing. In short, there was no one in the AP system to whom the confused and overwhelmed Los Angeles bureau could turn for the technical assistance required either to report the whole thing as a fraud or to bring it to the attention of the public in understandable terms and let the members of the public make up their own minds.

To the great benefit of all concerned, the subsequent disintegration of the Soviet Union and its Warsaw Pact has made it unlikely that anything resembling Desert Strike would be acted out "for real" in Western Europe. But the shadow of Desert Strike and the issues it raised hung over Desert Shield, the defensive phase of the 1990–91 Persian Gulf War, with a nightmarish immediacy.

If Iraq had elected to launch a massive armored assault, entirely within its means, against Saudi Arabia in late August or September of 1990, what would have been the U.S. response? A brigade of Saudi Arabian troops on the Kuwaiti border would have been surrounded within minutes. Would the United States have risked a nuclear strike, thus endangering those Saudi soldiers and other Saudi citizens in the border region? If not, was it prepared to accept the capture of thousands of lightly armed U.S. paratroopers and Marines just arriving via airlift and not yet "married up" with their heavy equipment?

The elaborate NATO procedures for dealing with such emergencies had been worked out through intricate international negotiations extending over decades. Even so, the Desert Strike test showed that, at the most optimistic, some six hours would be required to reach a decision. Yet there were no such procedures in place in the loosely organized Desert Shield alliance. There was no way to know in advance whether Saudi Arabia or any of the other Arab allies of the United States would tolerate the use of nuclear weapons against an Arab opponent, whatever the risks to the Saudis in the direct path of the Iraqi attack. There was no assurance that any of the European allies would sanction the use of nuclear weapons and almost no possibility of obtaining Japan's approval.

It would have taken days, more likely weeks or months, to resolve such questions, if they could be resolved at all. In the meantime the Iraqis would have settled the matter by occupying the Saudi ports and airfields and by blocking any further reinforcement except by amphibious and air assault. And they would have held as hostages against such an assault thousands of U.S. citizens as well as a captive Saudi population.

Only an instant unilateral decision by the U.S. president at the urging of the senior U.S. military officer on the scene could have applied nuclear firepower in time to stop an Iraqi invasion in its tracks. That would have devastated the alliance the United States was painfully building and would probably have solidified an anti-American Arab and fundamentalist Muslim alliance from northern Africa to central Asia.

In his drive to commit the United States irrevocably to military action in the Gulf before effective opposition could be marshalled in Congress, the U.S. president had no interest in permitting a public debate of such difficult questions. Once again, as in the presidential election of 1964, the inability of American journalism, in particular the AP, to bring the Desert Strike information and issues before the public in an understandable manner enabled an incumbent political party, in 1964, and a president of the opposite party, in 1990, to exclude from the public forum those issues with which they preferred not to deal, but which were of truly vital concern to the public.

On August 8–11, 1983, nineteen years after Desert Strike, in a federal district courtroom on the other side of the continent, it would be apparent that the AP was no nearer competence in dealing with the intricacies of national defense. Spread out on the public record in that courtroom was nothing less than the entire strategic planning process of the U.S. government.

During the campaign across France and Germany in 1945 General Dwight D. Eisenhower had learned to separate a group of his planners from the pressure of daily operations so that they could develop objectives and courses of action for the weeks and months ahead. In 1947, as part of the effort he and General George C. Marshall made to consolidate national military planning under a single National War College, Eisenhower, then chief of staff of the Army, created the Institute of Advanced Studies, with an eye toward incorporating it into the National War College when the last service war college, that of the Navy, was disestablished. Blocked in that by the Navy's refusal to relinquish its service war college, Eisenhower would try again, as president, by establishing a nascent long-range planning element as a separate part of the National Security Council. Eisenhower's successor as president John F. Kennedy, did away with that effort, preferring to rely on the advice of his brother and other trusted political associates.

That left the Army with an anomaly on its hands; what Eisenhower had intended to become a national long-range planning institute was now only an Army agency, its perspective inevitably limited by the Army's immediate bureaucratic and budgetary interests, or at least perceived interests. The Army would never learn how to deal with that problem, but in its age-old tradition its first instinct was to get it out of sight. That was accomplished by co-locating the institute with the Army War College when the Army felt forced to revive that institution, at Carlisle Barracks, Pennsylvania, in the face of the Navy's intransigence in refusing to accept the demise of the Naval War College.

What then followed is, to say the least, bizarre. One of the elements— eventually the sole surviving element—of the Institute of Advanced Studies was the study of national strategy, with a view toward mapping out and analyzing alternative long-range strategies, essentially what Eisenhower had in mind, but not just from an Army viewpoint. But the uniform characteristic of all the colonels selected to be the successive directors of the institute was that they had never participated through open publication or otherwise in the national strategic debate before appointment, did not participate during their tenure as director, and uniformly returned thereafter to the obscurity from which they had emerged. As a result of the less-than-inspired atmosphere that was created, the institute eventually became something of an elephant's graveyard, the last assignment for worthy colonels who had not quite made general, but who deserved a final, dignified professional resting place before retirement.

There were rare exceptions. In 1971–72, Colonel Thomas A. Lowe, one of the rare assignees with genuine strategic credentials as an interallied planner and negotiator, capped a succession of studies with a report that, among other things, accurately predicted the inability of National Guard combat brigades to mobilize with their assigned Active Army units during the Persian Gulf War, eighteen years later. But Lowe's team also identified a list of National Guard and Reserve units whose paid drill schedules could be reduced by some $500 million per year, in 1972 money, without jeopardizing their ability to mobilize when needed. That so alarmed the National Guard and Reserve establishment that it succeeded in placing two colonels full-time in what by then had been renamed the U.S. Army Strategic Studies Institute to make sure that no further disturbing proposals emerged therefrom. The War College acceded to that because it had fiscal problems of its own: The cost of the nine-month War College course was by then running close to $100,000 per student, something more than what it was then costing to put someone through four years at Harvard. That problem could be disguised only by spreading out the excess over a large number of non-resident corresponding students. Most of them would have to come from the National Guard and Reserve. Log-rolling is not confined to the U.S. Congress.

All parties but one gained, the loser being the taxpayer. Not only was the taxpayer denied a saving of some $10 billion in reduced National Guard and Reserve personnel accounts over the next twenty years, but also he or she had to pay an additional $2 million, conservatively estimated, to keep on duty in the Strategic Studies Institute those National Guard and Reserve watchdogs.

That would restore peace and decorum to the elephant's graveyard for another decade, except that another problem was slowly building beneath the placid surface. If the Army did not know what to do with the Strategic Studies Institute, there were Civil Service politicians in the institute's employ who did.

Hired initially as clerks and research assistants, the institute's civilians had gradually moved into the vacuum of leadership simply by default of the military. They at least knew the high-sounding academic jargon in which the output of largely useless studies had to be couched. Using, ironically, the brief fame Colonel Lowe's eventually aborted study had gained for the institute, the civilians had succeeded in that most time-honored of all bureaucratic fats—empire building, expanding the civilian work force by 100 percent and thereby, in equally time-honored fashion, creating a new base for further grade increases for at least selected members of the original staff.

If the generals in the Pentagon could not be bothered about such goings-on up at Carlisle, there were more junior officers who did know about it. When one of them got to be a general in the right place, the roof at Carlisle finally fell in, or so it appeared at first.

The Army's solution was to fire the entire fifteen-person "professional" civilian staff of the Strategic Studies Institute—all of the original staff, plus those added during the 1972 expansion. That was to be accomplished by certifying to the Office of Personnel Management, custodians of the federal Civil Service system, that the fifteen positions were no longer needed. At the same time, however, and by another route the Army sought to establish nine replacement positions in the Excepted Civil Service, outside the long-term merit system. In this attempt, however, it failed to recognize that, if experts in nothing else, the creators of the "empire" in the Strategic Studies Institute were experts in Civil Service regulations. What the Army had done was patently unlawful, and that is what landed everybody concerned in a federal district courtroom in Harrisburg in August 1983 before an examiner from the investigative arm of the Civil Service.

The Harrisburg bureau of the AP had known for no less than seven years previous that something was seriously wrong in the Army's domain at Carlisle, fifteen miles distant. It had been informed in detail by what would now be called "whistleblowers" who had run into dead ends in terms of all of the administrative and inspector general avenues open to them within the Army. But the AP staffers were visibly overwhelmed by the complexity of the issues, and they had no one, either in the AP's New York headquarters or in Washington, to whom they could turn for assistance. No one from the AP showed up to cover the three days of hearings, even though the principal AP subscriber in Harrisburg, the Newhouse chain *Patriot-News*, had also been fully informed of the hearings and of the important, national-level issues involved.

What were involved, it turned out, were much more momentous issues than the aborted National Guard and Reserve savings, the empire building, and the years of accumulated waste. What had precipitated the attempted mass firing, Army witnesses testified, was panic in the Army staff in Washington over Reagan administration plans to build a 600-ship Navy, money for which must eventually come from the sale, so to speak, of the Army's "crown jewels," its European garrisons. So, according to documents placed in evidence, high-ranking Army officials had decided to breathe life into what they described as their "third-rate think tank" in order to hire civilian academics who would somehow come up with the ideas necessary to sink the 600-ship Navy before it got fairly started. They hit on the Excepted Civil Service as a means of keeping the academics on their toes by holding over them the threat of being let go, a much simpler process under the excepted system than under the merit system. Along the way the Army witnesses allowed that some of the original fifteen employees were "salvageable" and might eventually be included in the new system.

Both the Navy and the Air Force had copied the Army Strategic Studies Institute idea. In varying ways many of the flaws that had corrupted the original Eisenhower concept also had been copied. As a result, there is probably no other public document, classified or unclassified, that describes the flaws of the internal defense management system that led to the enormous overfunding of military budgets during the Reagan era so completely and so clearly as does the record of those three days of hearings. A retired Army master sergeant who sat through all three days of the hearings remarked ruefully at the end, "Now I know how we lost the Vietnam War."[7]

No one else in the country would know, however, because the AP, which can cope with stories about the purchase by military officials of $600 toilet seats and $45 hammers, has neither the organization nor the training to comprehend the stories that, given timely exposure, could lead to the savings of millions and ultimately billions of dollars. The taxpayer was the ultimate loser, again, in the Army's clumsy effort to restructure its Strategic Studies Institute, in that the Army got the nine Excepted Civil Service "spaces" it was seeking, but it was required to take back all fifteen of the original staff, "salvageable" or not. The level of performance overall has continued as before, but at a cost over a third higher.

The other principal wire services—United Press International and Reuters—are even less well equipped to deal with the complexities of national and international security affairs.

What was then only United Press (UP) was founded in 1907 by E. W. Scripps of what would become the Scripps-Howard newspaper chain because the AP's subscribers could then deny the services of the wire service to rivals, a practice later outlawed by the U.S. Supreme Court. In 1958 UP merged with a Hearst-chain wire service, International News Service, to form United Press International (UPI). After a long chain of financial losses, UPI was sold by Scripps to a group of private investors in 1982, and it has been staggering to successive financial crises ever since, filing for bankruptcy in 1991.

Throughout its history, UPI has focused on "scooping" its larger rival, helping to generate in the AP the same sort of focus on immediacy rather than comprehension. This formula would produce an international disaster during the 1968 Tet Offensive in Vietnam.

Both of the major wire services have prided themselves on covering "the rat holes that others don't bother to watch."[8] Like the AP, UPI never assigned more than two reporters, both at the Pentagon, to cover U.S. national defense, worldwide, the same level of coverage accorded the Department of Agriculture.

Reuters was organized in 1851 by a group of newspapers in Britain, Ireland, Australia, and New Zealand. It remains British-owned and thereby carries the burden of the Official Secrets Act. In the United States Reuters had concentrated, at least until the early 1980s, on business and financial news. In 1981 Reuters sought to purchase the weakening UPI, a merger that would have created a world journalistic enterprise rivaling the AP. However, Reuters abandoned the effort in the same year, leaving unresolved the question of how to deal with a major U.S. news-gathering agency that was subject, through the Official Secrets Act, to at least indirect control by a foreign government.

Growing pressure on regional U.S. newspapers for national and international coverage of greater depth than the wire services have traditionally offered has led major newspapers—principally the *New York Times* and a joint *Washington Post–Los Angeles Times*–(New York) *Newsday* network—to offer their own wire services. The result has been to discourage even further any AP efforts to provide reports and news analysis beyond its traditional fire-alarm level. Thus, the weaknesses of the major newspapers become increasingly the weaknesses of all, in particular with respect to weak and inadequate coverage of national defense.

Given that most of the American public gets most of its news from television and that television relies on the principal U.S. newspapers and the wire services for the greater part of the news it broadcasts, what assurance does that provide that the public is obtaining accurate, timely advance information as to the why and how of U.S. military wars and lesser military operations?

Are the twelve full-time journalists assigned to the Pentagon building by the networks, the national newspapers, and the wire services, none of them with specialized training or background for the assignment, sufficient to provide the American public with a comprehensive, timely, accurate assessment of the value received from a worldwide military establishment with an average active-duty strength of two million men and women?

If the answer to both of those questions with respect to routine, peacetime coverage is, to say the least, "doubtful," what is the assurance of comprehensive, timely, and accurate coverage in time of war?

NOTES

1. Richard Leonard, correspondence with author, January–February, 1964.

2. "The Associated Press: How It Came to Be and What It Has Become," promotional pamphlet, The Associated Press, New York, p. 2.

3. Quoted by Deirdre Carmody, "The Associated Press Is Developing Broader Perception of What Is News," *New York Times*, 1 June 1976.

4. Untitled and undated news release, The Associated Press, New York.

5. Phil G. Goulding, *Confirm or Deny* (New York: Harper & Row, 1970), 104–5.

6. Unable to obtain an assignment from Leonard or any other major editor, the author obtained an active-duty assignment as an Army public affairs officer in the Joint Exercise Desert Strike Information Office. In that capacity he served as one of a two-man team assigned to write the twice-daily exercise communiques.

7. Stated to the author, 11 August 1983.

8. Peter Edson, "Wire Services in Washington," in *The Press in Washington*, ed. Ray Eldon Hiebert (New York: Dodd, Mead & Co., 1967), 45.

6

The Magazines

Is there enough information on the public record and available to the ordinary citizen at any given time to enable him or her to determine how well or how poorly the U.S. defense establishment is performing in peace—and is prepared to perform in war?

The answer to that question is an unequivocal "yes."

By focusing total concentration on military developments for over forty years, the author has been able to anticipate every major trend, and every major weakness, in U.S. national defense and, where cooperative editors could be found, to publish such findings. Access to the highest levels of classified information during periods of military service and civilian government employment interspersed over those forty years confirmed that nothing held by the government undermined or contradicted judgments drawn from the open, unclassified sources.

That is one of the glories of the society the Founding Fathers bequeathed to us.

But how many ordinary Americans have the time to spend at least an hour reading the *New York Times* every day, 365 days a year, plus at least half a day each week reviewing the past week's *Wall Street Journal, Washington Post,* and *Christian Science Monitor* and at least spot-checking the *Chicago Tribune* and *Los Angeles Times,* plus monitoring major defense hearings broadcast on the C-Span network? How many can acquire beforehand the active-duty military experience and the professional military education required to make sense of what is read and keep that experience and education reasonably up to date by reading closely each month the privately published, but quasi-official *U.S. Naval Institute Proceedings* and *Air Force* magazine and the privately published, and entirely unofficial, weekly *Army Times* newspaper and monthly *Armed Forces Journal International?*

In truth, the process should be stated the other way around. Active-duty experience is not the only way to acquire an understanding of what national defense is all about, but it is the most reliable, and in some ways the easiest.

Homer Lea (1876–1912), the only true military genius the United States has produced to date and (with Alfred Thayer Mahan) its premier military writer, could not have gained admission to any part of the U.S. armed services. He was a hunchback, among numerous other afflictions. But his books, primarily *The Valor of Ignorance* and *The Day of the Saxon*, mapped out all of the major military relationships of the twentieth century, including both world wars and the struggle between the United States and the Soviet Union for supremacy in the Cold War. He achieved that, however, only through enormous intellectual and physical exertions, the former far beyond the capacity of most ordinary mortals and the latter far beyond the limits to which anything but powerful intellect and will could have driven a frail and twisted physique.

Ideally, a combination of both enlisted and commissioned officer service is required to gain an understanding of how the military bureaucracy works. Which branch of service is less important, at least at the introductory level. That means three to five years, a big chunk out of a person's life, but, for a journalist determined to understand the military, an experience far more important than graduate school.

Formal military education is available to anyone willing and physically and mentally qualified to serve in the National Guard or Reserve. Even without formal affiliation, such education is or could easily be made available by means of the excellent correspondence courses administered by all of the armed forces. Completion of the command and general staff college course, the next to the highest level of formal military instruction, is the minimum required to gain an overview. It would be a fairly simple matter to incorporate that into a graduate program at a civilian university aimed at producing specialists in defense journalism.

From that base of practical experience and academic instruction the military magazines and other periodicals, available to anyone for the price of subscription, become intelligible. The monthly *U.S. Naval Institute Proceedings* is far and away the premier U.S. professional military journal, albeit with obvious limitations in that it presents almost exclusively a Navy and Marine Corps point of view. *Air Force* magazine is the journal of the Air Force Association, built on heavy aviation and space industry support. The magazine has benefited from a succession of first-rate editors, but it treads very carefully around the interests of its industrial patrons. A succession of first-rate editors has also given *Army Times* premier standing over the several official and quasi-official publications focused on the Army. It depends to a large extent on unit subscriptions, however, and that limits somewhat its

scope in dealing with stories that bring into question the continued usefulness
of particular units or entire elements of the Army force structure. *Armed
Forces Journal International* has become increasingly oriented in recent
years toward international military sales, but it still presents articles of importance to U.S. defense policy and national strategy by competent authors.

A wide range of more specialized military publications, official and unofficial, all of them unclassified, provides even more detailed insight into
the workings of U.S. national defense. Another group of publications dealing
with foreign military establishments is available in English.

The trained reader who studies assiduously the principal components of
U.S. professional military literature and who is aware at least generally of
what is available in the more specialized literature is then in a position to
understand and evaluate what appears day in and day out in the *New York
Times* and the rest of the national press. What, then, of *Time, Newsweek,*
and *U.S. News and World Report?*

The great strength of the news magazines is that they appear weekly,
rather than daily. In theory, that should enable them to provide a perspective
that newspapers cannot achieve, working under daily deadlines. That has
meaning, however, only if the people who are charged with providing the
perspective have the training and the means to exploit the increased time.

The weekly national and international news magazine should perform
another important function—providing, in succinct, readable form, depth
and background for the reader who does not have ready access to the major
national dailies or the time to read them.

A year after the Persian Gulf War of 1990–91 ended, an assemblage of
U.S. News and World Report writers still could not get straight what had
happened, even with all of the relevant information on the public record.
"The Marines began the ground campaign, and they set the pace for it . . . ,"
the *U.S. News* team reported in the January 20, 1992, issue.

That is an astonishing statement. It is no reflection on the prowess of the
Marines to record that they were still in Kuwait when the war ended, but
U.S. and French air cavalry on the western flank, far inland from the Marines, had moved hundreds of miles, had overcome or isolated substantial
numbers of Iraqi troops, and was in position to block the withdrawal of the
entire Iraqi army if a cease-fire had not been ordered.

The function the Marines had performed would have been understandable
to anyone who had served as a private in an infantry squad, or who had at
least observed and understood squad training exercises. That is, the Marines
had been the "fixing force," holding large numbers of Iraqis in place, while
the "maneuvering force"—the U.S. and French air cavalry—swung around
into the enemy's rear.

Indeed, the writers missed entirely the significance of the constrained,
but still impressive, "support" role played by the attack helicopter. They
missed as well the enormous significance of the power demonstrated when

six attack helicopter battalions were massed into what amounted to a provisional air cavalry brigade in the closing hours of the war, devastating Iraqi columns fleeing across the Al Hammar causeway and, in effect, ending the role of the heavy tank in modern warfare.

That January 20, 1992, *U.S. News* article was described as the précis of the book *Triumph Without Victory: The Unreported History of the Persian Gulf War*, authored, so it was claimed, "by an award-winning staff of *U.S. News and World Report*." Whoever gave them that award should take it back.

Not only were the authors unable to properly assess the relationship between a mainly dismounted Marine force moving, at best, at two-and-one-half miles per hour (the standard pace of the infantry) and air cavalry units moving at near one hundred miles per hour, but also they fell hook, line, and sinker for the official "line": that heavy armored formations had won the war. That derived, doubtlessly, from the fact that the commanding general of one of the heavy divisions, the 24th Mechanized Division, had taken a senior *U.S. News* writer under his wing, but had not revealed to him that the 24th's tanks and armored personnel carriers were being led by fuel trucks trying to keep up with the attack helicopters and other air cavalry units that were heading the allied assault and were seven hours to three days ahead of the 24th and other heavy armored formations.

The result is that the article, and presumably the book, focuses mainly on the huge heavy armored forces whose de facto role was to mop up behind the air cavalry. It totally escaped the writers that for all intents and purposes the war was over when the Third Brigade of the heli-borne 101st Airborne Division established itself on one of the major Iraqi escape routes, while other heliborne units backed by attack helicopters and Air Force and Navy fighters prepared to block all of the remaining routes if the cease-fire had not intervened.

No army, least of all an army of heavy armored vehicles depending on huge quantities of fuel and thousands of tons per day of ammunition and spare parts, can survive the severing of its logistical system, yet that is what the attack helicopters were in the process of doing in conjunction with Air Force and Navy fighter-bombers and attack aircraft. The spectacular armored battles that occurred as the allied juggernaut moved forward were impressive, but they had no more relationship to the outcome of the war than did the charge of the Light Brigade to the outcome of the Crimean War.

Except for a graphic, the reader would never have known from the January 20, 1992 *U.S. News* article that the 101st Airborne Division was already in the process of cutting the Iraqis' logistical lifeline when the cease-fire was ordered, with units in position to effect a far more complete entrapment if operations had not been halted. In terms of text, the reader was informed only that "The Desert Storm operations plan called for the XVIII Airborne Corps," of which the 101st was the principal maneuver element, "to drive east, close the Basra Pocket on the north and trap the Republican Guard divisions retreating from the [allied armored assault]." That the air cavalry concept—over thirty years in the making—had proven stunningly successful in putting the American and French forces in position to "close the Basra Pocket" was unnoticed and unreported by the reporting team.

The *U.S. News* team then introduced another misconception, destined to cause endless confusion: "The cease fire prevented [the heavy allied armored forces] from completing [entrapment] and allowed the bulk of the Republican Guard forces to escape with their weapons."

When that had first appeared in similar terms in the March 16, 1992, *U.S. News and World Report*, Tom Donnelly, editor of *Army Times*, noted in print that much of the fallacy derived from the failure of the national press, again with all of the pertinent information on the public record, to sort out what constituted the Republican Guard. As verified by all of the primary documents available in terms of U.S. unit after-action reports and interviews with participants at battalion command level and higher, all of the three armored divisions that were the core of the Republican Guard were devastated. That resulted in part because relentless bombing preceded the ground campaign and in at least equal part because helicopter gunships blocked the escape routes until called off by the cease-fire, with large portions destroyed by the follow-on allied armored units. But because residual units of the Iraqi army had subsequently proved effective in suppressing revolts in southern and northern Iraq, not only *U.S. News*, but also just about all of U.S. national journalism assumed that it was true that the major units of the Republican Guard had, indeed, escaped.

In that is exposed one of the worst disservices all of American national journalism does its readers, viewers, and listeners. The general assignment reporter, including the general assignment reporter whose exposure to the military consists mainly of a two- or three-year assignment to the Pentagon, grasps at catchwords to delude himself or herself and the reader, viewer, or listener into thinking that complex issues can be understood in such terms.

An enhanced radiation weapon developed under the threat of a massed Soviet armored attack in Central Europe became the "neutron bomb, designed to kill people but not destroy property." That the people the weapon was designed to kill or disable were tank crews and the "saved" property now inoperative armored vehicles never caught up with the "neutron bomb" scare words. And the emotion infused by journalists into those words blocked public understanding that the alternatives were nuclear weapons with far more catastrophic effects, all of which remained in the arsenals.

"Star Wars," journalism's translation of the Strategic Defense Initiative into the vernacular of a public it does not believe capable of understanding more involved terminology, is, to date, the worst example of the genre. If ever there was a program that demands careful, rational debate, it is this one. With nuclear weapons technology proliferating throughout the world the threat of nuclear blackmail is becoming steadily greater, notwithstanding the end of the Cold War. If there is some way to increase the element of doubt in the mind of the potential blackmailer that a small arsenal of nuclear weapons and missile delivery systems can hold the world hostage, then the evolution of even a marginally effective anti-missile defense system is that hope.

The anti-missile systems that have been under development with increasing success since the 1960s have nothing to do with the stars. Not even the moon. To have described the continuing effort as "Star Wars" was to have virtually eliminated rational public debate. The element of ridicule in the term, drawn from motion picture fantasies, is immediately apparent. Its adoption by the press and its routine use throughout American journalism, led by its bellwether, the *New York Times*, make claims to objectivity and professionalism a travesty.

"Republican Guard" was made to order for journalists accustomed to covering up their lack of depth by reliance on catchwords, and in that they fell into a trap of their own making. As Donnelly of *Army Times* would point out, fixation on the words, rather than on the reality, precluded careful analysis of what the term meant and what it did not.

Based on information available in open sources before the Gulf War began and confirmed by all the data compiled during the war—and available to the *U.S. News* reporting team if they had known where to look and what they were looking at—Donnelly noted that "Too much has been made of the centrality of the Republican Guard to Saddam [Hussein]'s power. The four-brigade Baghdad Division seems to [have been] the original . . . Praetorian Guard. But as the Republican Guard grew it was simply impossible to conduct the kind of security review necessary to ensure unswerving loyalty. At the conclusion of the Iran-Iraq War [preceding the Gulf War] . . . battalion commanders were interchangeable among the units of the Republican Guard and the regular heavy army formations."[1]

Not only *U.S. News and World Report*, but also CBS News got the impression that the bulk of the Republican Guard got away. They arrived at this conclusion by a process of backward reasoning from the success of the Saddam Hussein government in putting down the Shiite rebellion in southern Iraq and the Kurdish rebellion in northern Iraq immediately after the Gulf War cease-fire. Surely, the *U.S. News* team and CBS seem to have reasoned, only the well-equipped, well-trained Republican Guard could have been so efficient.

In fact, it does not take a great deal of efficiency for an army equipped with tanks and attack helicopters to defeat men and women armed only with rifles. As events demonstrated, the remnants of Saddam's army, however badly mauled, had more than enough firepower left to accomplish that. Included among those remnants, as identified to Donnelly by his Army sources, were "about 30 percent" of the fighting power of the Hammurabai

Republican Guard armored division and "40 to 50 percent" of the Medinah division. Donnelly says that the Tawakalna division, the third major unit of the Republican Guard's heavy armor core, "was destroyed in detail by the [U.S.] 2d Armored Cavalry Regiment and the [U.S.] 3d Armored Division."[2]

All of that tallies exactly with the wide range of after-action reports and interviews with individual participants reviewed by the author, a range of sources far too diverse to have been coordinated to concoct some sort of elaborate lie. All of those sources were available to *U.S. News*, CBS News, and anyone else who was willing to travel extensively outside of Washington and who knew what he or she was looking for and where to look. Months after the war, however, a poll of those sources revealed that they had been contacted by only one low-ranking news magazine research assistant.

Newsweek did no better than did *U.S. News*. In the same week—January 20, 1992—in which *U.S. News* confounded itself and its readers with a totally misreported version of the Gulf War, *Newsweek* did the same, reporting the defeat of the Iraqis as the product of "a daring armored assault." Yet the unchallenged record shows that the "daring armored assault" never came within seven hours of the advancing U.S. and French attack helicopters and, indeed, was led not by tanks, but by refueling trucks racing to keep up with the helicopters. All that was possible, *Newsweek* reported, because the allied forces that performed the spectacular, and decisive, flanking movement were "unopposed."

Yet the staff journals of the XVIII Airborne Corps, under which the flanking movement was conducted, record that during the week prior to the start of the allied ground offensive "two deep attack missions were ordered in support of the 6th French (Light) Division . . . The attack [by two attack helicopter battalions] began at 0200 18 February, concentrating on chemical-capable artillery and . . . armor units. . . . [Iraqi] air defense artillery was eliminated. . . . " That set the stage for a second attack, on February 20. "A company of armored personnel carriers was located and destroyed," according to the staff journals, "as were numerous trucks and bunkers. . . . The major threats to the French attack had been neutralized."

The U.S. and French after-action reports, all available to anyone who sought them out, showed further Iraqi resistance as the flanking movement on the western flank progressed, all of it either overwhelmed and suppressed by attack helicopter assault or bypassed by the helicopters and overcome by follow-on U.S. and French armored units. If the U.S. and French advance was "unopposed," it was only because the Iraqi forces that sought to stand in the way were destroyed, not the usual meaning of "unopposed."

To compound its own and the reader's confusion, *Newsweek* reported in the same January 20, 1992 issue that "The 101st Airborne was scheduled to help close [the Al Hammar] causeway. It never got there. . . . " If that is true, credit one of the assault helicopter battalion commanders with a vivid imagination.

"As we approached the causeway," the air cavalry commander told an interviewer, "it was so dark [from burning oil wells] we had to go from day TV to FLIR [Forward Looking Infrared] to be able to see. . . . At the point where we moved up to where we could see the causeway, the visibility was probably less than 300 meters and it was just pure black smoke. . . . The first thing we saw [in the infrared scope] was an SA–6 [anti-aircraft missile] locked onto us . . . [and we] shot him with a 30 millimeter cannon. . . .

"The causeway," seen through eyes that *Newsweek* says "never got there," "was at least two lanes south and two lanes north. . . . We shot up a lot of vehicles here [and continued until] we had serviced just about all the targets we could acquire on the causeway itself. . . .

"At this point," says the air cavalry commander concerning the "daring armored assault," "the closest friendly force was 75 kilometers away on the ground . . . certainly it would have taken an armor division a day to get there. . . . This was purely a helicopter fight. . . . "

It was not until March 2 that the first elements of the nearest heavily armored allied force, the U.S. 24th Mechanized Division, arrived on the scene. This was three days after the attack helicopter battalions had filled the causeway and its approaches with the wreckage of hundreds of Iraqi vehicles.

Why did the *Newsweek* team, grandly assembled from "Washington, London and New York," get things so wrong with a year to work on the story and all sources open to anyone who knew where to look and what questions to ask? Because none of the major weekly news magazines thinks coverage of national defense is important enough to train and employ people over the long term who know where to look and what questions to ask.

It is all spelled out in the masthead, the list of editorial and corporate titles published every week. *U.S. News and World Report* proclaims as its priorities "Business, Science and Society, News You Can Use, Investigative Projects and Special Reports." At the next lower level are "Special Correspondents" (i.e., stringers) for El Salvador, Panama, Britain, Germany, Czechoslovakia, Israel, Kenya, South Africa, and Thailand. The first indication of interest in the defense story appears at priority level three—"Contributing Editors" (i.e., people whose names are nice to have on the masthead and to whom a telephone call might be made if time permits). Even here, at this remote distance from the editorial inner sanctum, the interest in the defense story is implicit, rather than explicit. That is, only the initiated recognize John Keegan as a military historian and James Fallows and Henry Trewhitt as journalists who have covered military stories from time to time.

Far, far down in a list of editors (general, associate, and assistant), "senior writers," "senior editorial assistants," and "editorial assistants," *Newsweek* finally acknowledges—also implicitly, rather than explicitly—a remote priority for defense reporting in the person of a "contributing editor," retired Army Colonel David Hackworth. How remote Hackworth is from the editorial mainstream is made plain in the muddled January 20, 1992, Gulf War anniversary story. He is not listed among the writers "in Washington, London and New York" who contributed to the main story. His name appears as the last of four in a separate news analysis "box" that somehow concluded, 'The [Gulf War] was a desert cakewalk, not a template for future conflicts . . . ," a reasonable conclusion for anyone who had managed to avoid noticing the role of the U.S. 101st Airborne Division and the French air cavalry in beginning the entrapment of the entire Iraqi army in Kuwait and southern Iraq and the spectacular performance of the attack helicopter battalions everywhere they were employed.

The extent to which Colonel Hackworth participated in the earlier analysis is brought into question by a commentary he finally got to write under his own byline at the end of the Gulf War article. "On the day of the cease fire," Hackworth wrote, "the 101st Airborne Division was ready to launch an air assault on 'Objective Thomas,' northwest of Basra, and close the back door." That's at least getting somewhere close to the facts.

If anyone from *Newsweek* had bothered to visit Fort Campbell, Kentucky, to which the 101st Airborne Division had returned after the war, the division briefing officer would have cheerfully related that "The 3rd Brigade [of the 101st] . . . had blocked Highway 8 [the Iraqi escape route running west from Basra]. . . . The Iraqis stopped trying to move West and began to try to escape . . . by moving North. . . . [On order from the XVIII Corps commander] we adjusted plans and had the 2d Brigade seize a new forward operating base, 'Viper.' . . . In less than 24 hours . . . AH–64 [attack helicopter] battalions were attacking into Engagement Area Thomas [blocking the last—northern—escape route from Basra]. . . . The AH–64s destroyed numerous vehicles and anti-aircraft guns [in Engagement Area Thomas] and even did some damage on the bridge across the Euphrates."

Indeed, as *Newsweek* had finally managed to mention in a sort of backhand way, the 101st Division briefing stated that "We issued orders to the 1st Brigade to air assault the following day to block Engagement Area Thomas [but] just before the attack the ceasefire was called." In short. *Newsweek* was only slightly less wrong about what went on along the escape routes from Basra than it had been in reporting that the six AH–64 attack helicopter battalions that raked the causeway leading north from Kuwait "never got there."

While it was true that the cease-fire stopped an infantry and artillery brigade of the 101st from physically blocking the northern escape route through Engagement Area Thomas, the division's principal firepower—its attack helicopter battalions—was already fully engaged in the area, the product of a phenomenal advance over hundreds of miles in the time it took the armored divisions to move a small fraction of that distance. Thus, while "the daring armored assault" on which *Newsweek* had focused the reader's attention was three days away from catching up with the massed attack helicopter assault at the causeway leading north from Kuwait, it was at least a week away from catching up with the 101st forces already deployed in the Euphrates River valley. And the walking infantry of the Marines, described by *U.S. News and World Report* as having "set the pace" for the ground war, were much farther behind than that.

Time's priorities as proclaimed in the masthead are generally identical to those of *U.S. News* and of *Newsweek*. There is a "Diplomatic Correspondent" and a "National Political Correspondent." Although neither national nor international security affairs rate such distinction, initiates to the defense story would note, up to the point when he was appointed as an official of the Clinton Administration, the presence, as "Editor-at-Large," of Strobe Talbott. Talbott's area of defense-related expertise, however, is entirely in the esoteric, primarily political and economic, realm of nuclear deterrence theories and disarmament once described by former Secretary of Defense James Schlesinger as more "theological" than military. In general, in the view of staff members of Boston University's Center for Defense Journalism, *Timer* seems to have avoided such embarrassments as befell *U.S. News* and *Newsweek* in the misreported Gulf War anniversary stories simply by avoiding such attempts at close reporting entirely, concentrating on commentary, by far the safer realm.

Throughout the entire period since World War II, defense reporting by the three major news weeklies can best be described as erratic.

With Strobe Talbott giving high visibility to its logo in the academic and political realms, *Time* saw no need to invest time and money in coverage of what its editors apparently took to be more mundane aspects of defense. Even in the nuclear field, however, that proved to be a mistake. The young man *Time* sent out to cover the crucially important Joint Exercise Desert Strike battlefield nuclear test in 1964 was plainly bemused by all that he saw and heard during the day he spent in the desert. Back in his air-conditioned Los Angeles office on the day the maneuver moved into high gear he wrote, and *Time* published, the same sort of vapid "color" piece that the wire services were turning out when they bothered to send anything at all. Dependent on the wire services once their Los Angeles man returned home, *Time* missed entirely both the relationship of the maneuver to long-term problems of nuclear weapons control and its more immediate relationship to major issues in the 1964 presidential campaign.

Seventeen years later, *Time*'s conception of what it takes to cover national defense had made no progress whatever. "A Letter from the Publisher," concerning a July 27, 1981, cover story on the status of the U.S. military told the reader that "Chicago correspondent Patricia Delaney, who as a child visited uncles who were resident officers at Fort Sheridan and the Great Lakes Naval Training Center, returned to both bases. . . . To assess sophisticated modern weaponry, Correspondent Jerry Hannifin not only talked with Army generals . . . but also went up for a test ride in an F–18." In following Defense Secretary Caspar Weinberger around for five months, "Correspondent Roberto Suro [learned] that the future is the 'outyears' and that battles no longer have front lines but instead have FEBAs—Forward Edge Battle Areas . . . ," terms by then in use since the early 1960s. Only Johanna McGeary over at Congress had managed to get beyond this kindergarten level of reporting. Confronting the looming Reagan defense buildup budgets, McGeary concluded that "The American public . . . [has] no idea as yet what the social and economic cost will be."

And that pattern has never changed: reasonable competence in coverage of Congress; except for an individual reporter or editor now and then, general incompetence in coverage of national defense. "Our military correspondent," a former *Time* Washington bureau chief boasted of the one and only *Time* correspondent, out of some 400, worldwide, who are assigned to cover national defense, "can, and has covered a National Open Golf tournament."[3]

For some twenty years, *Newsweek* had a competent military journalist, Lloyd Norman, but he was not replaced, with results that speak for themselves in the botched Persian Gulf War analysis.

U.S. News has a long, if sporadic, history of trying to patch in senior retired military officers, an example that *Newsweek* has now begun to copy. One problem with that "solution" is that the higher the rank, the less inclined they are to "demean" themselves by dealing on an equal level with sources, especially military sources, much junior to themselves. That was plainly evident during the reign of one such senior officer at *U.S. News* during the 1960s. Over the two years of a major controversy, Department of Defense public affairs officers found themselves dealing with no less than five different junior *U.S. News* staffers, each as ignorant as his predecessor of the substance of the controversy, because "the general" did not deign to become involved.

For a time following the demise of the *Washington Evening Star, U.S. News* acquired the only true military journalist it has ever employed in the person of Orr Kelly, the *Star*'s competent Pentagon reporter. But *U.S. News* then recruited yet another soon-to-be-retired officer in the person of Colonel Harry Summers whose book on the Vietnam War, *On Strategy*, had delighted the world of journalism by its careful avoidance of any suggestion that the performance of the press in Vietnam had been anything but competent and purely objective.

Concerning his then new career in journalism, Summers told the *Harrisburg*, Pennsylvania *Patriot-News*[4] that "he's going to cling to a bit of the past. He said he insisted his byline list him as 'Colonel.' " Summers's attitude toward his new colleagues was reverential: "The media types who hang out in the Pentagon and the White House and Congress, he said, have too much moxie. He said they'd beat him every time." In deference to that he would concentrate on analysis, not on reporting.

Summers expressed heartfelt gratitude to then Army Chief of Staff Edward C. Meyer, the former commandant of the Army War College; Dewitt C.

Smith, Jr.; and then War College Commandant Jack N. Merritt, all of them deeply involved at the moment in newsworthy controversies. Among these were the exclusion of thousands of Army women from assignments for which they had enlisted in good faith;[5] violations of the Civil Service merit system appointment and promotion system; a long succession of race, sex, and age discrimination cases;[6] the use of Army War College facilities as a research source for the Republican National Committee;[7] and the use of threats of psychiatric "consultation" to force discontinuance of the discrimination actions and to suppress public knowledge of all of the preceding. Summers was awarded the title of, and continually identified himself in print as, "a Distinguished Fellow of the Army War College."

Can anyone so deeply and publicly attached to a public institution and to high officials in that institution be depended on to tell the reader when that institution, or those officials, has failed? Not likely.

Not cited directly by Summers, but underlying all that he said in the interview is a much deeper problem. Partly because of the nomadic nature of military life, partly by preference, career military families form virtually no close ties outside of the military. By deliberate choice, most seek to continue that close association by settling in areas where those lifetime friendships can be maintained in an equally close retired military community. No one knows better than the career military wife that the penalty for criticism of the military institution, in particular of high-ranking members of that institution, is instant and everlasting ostracism. For those many career military families with children who have followed them into the regular military service, involvement of a parent in public criticism of the military can have fatal career consequences.

No career retired officer-become-journalist, no matter what he learns of military malfeasance or how strongly he may feel about the incompetence of a high-ranking officer, can avoid thinking about the consequences to his family if he reports what he knows in print or on the air.

It should be equally obvious that a job in journalism, in particular at the national level, presents an ideal opportunity to cover up embarrassments one may have left behind in a military career. The higher the rank, the more likely the existence of such problems—and the greater the temptation.

To these personal burdens that the retired career military officer carries over into journalism must be added very heavy professional burdens.

No one attains the grade of Army, Air Force, or Marine Corps colonel or Navy captain without having become deeply committed to a particular professional structure—the services themselves—and substructures within the services. That service loyalty, and the point of view shaped by twenty to thirty years of training in one or more of the service subcultures, is apparent in one way or another in the work of every senior retired officer who has ever subsequently entered journalism, even among the very few who sought to distance themselves from their previous profession.

Newsweek's Colonel Hackworth, whose dissent from Army policies and the national strategy in Vietnam put him almost totally beyond the service pale, is about as extreme an example as is ever likely to be found of the trained officer without personal or professional attachment to his past. Yet, called upon to assess the role of women in the military, Hackworth could address the subject only as an infantryman, riveted by his personal combat experiences and unable to fully address an age in which dexterity in manipulation of electronic controls is of at least equal military consequence to the physical strength required of the infantry soldier. That female helicopter pilots performed effectively in the Persian Gulf War, while, by and large, the infantry brought up the rear in trucks and armored personnel carriers, simply did not fit in with Hackworth's lifetime mindset, and so was dismissed out of hand.

Faced, in the early 1980s, with the Reagan administration's plans for a huge military buildup, editors and Washington bureau chiefs, notably of the *Los Angeles Times* and the *New York Times*, turned to specialized defense periodicals for reporters who at least were familiar with the names of the programs and the Defense budgetary structure, albeit in almost all cases entirely lacking in familiarity with the U.S. armed forces outside of Washington.

Specialized periodicals, notably such as the Army, Navy, and the Air Force *Times* weekly newspapers and the monthly *Aviation Week and Space Technology*, continue to train entry-level and advanced journalists in the defense field. But with what the greater part of American journalism plainly takes to be the dawn of everlasting peace in the wake of the decline of the Soviet Union, those specialty periodicals and their staffs, to the extent they survive at all, seem certain to live in a world apart from such as *Time*, *Newsweek*, and *U.S. News and World Report*, in all of which the general assignment reporter continues to reign supreme. Whatever the continuing economic benefit to management and the shareholders of this arrangement, the fiascoes of Gulf War coverage published by *Newsweek* and *U.S. News*, and by *Time* through omission, make it plain that it is the reader who is the loser.

NOTES

1. Tom Donnelly, "Iraq's Heavy Forces Were Dismembered," *Army Times*, 23 March 1992, p. 37.

2. Ibid.

3. John L. Steele, "The News Magazines in Washington," in *The Press in Washington*, ed. Ray Eldon Hiebert (New York: Dodd, Mead & Co., 1967), chap. 5.

4. Roger Doran, "Colonel Turns into a Journalist," *Harrisburg*, (Pa.), *Evening News*, 3 September 1985, p. C14.

5. The conclusions were the result of a "Women in the Army" study, hastily engineered at the onset of the Reagan administration, apparently in the expectation

that the new administration could be counted on to stop, and reverse, the "inroads" of women into traditional men-only service roles.

6. These were described to the civilian work force at the U.S. Army War College by Major General, later Lieutenant General, Robert G. Yerkes during his tenure as War College commandant, 1974–75.

7. This was reported to the inspector general when the author began to receive calls from the Republican National Committee for a contract professor in the same office who then routinely reported to these callers the products of publicly funded research conducted at the War College. The same professor was actively supporting a postretirement job for the then War College commandant at his home university. The inspector general concluded that supplying publicly funded research to the Republican National Committee was permissible because the professor was only a contract employee of a consulting firm paid by the committee.

7

Vietnam: The Watershed

Try as one might, Hanson W. Baldwin commented in an interview concerning his long career as military correspondent of the *New York Times*, it is impossible to separate coverage of military affairs from politics.[1]

For Baldwin that was a vast understatement of the bitter rear-guard action he had fought during his last decade at the *Times*. It was a struggle born in equal parts of the *Times*'s deep commitment to the Kennedy political dynasty and, paradoxically, of the *Times*'s growing opposition to what would become President John F. Kennedy's principal legacy, the Vietnam War.

The history of that internal struggle is told in thousands of internal *Times* documents deposited by Baldwin in the Sterling Library at Yale University, with important additional background in a series of oral history interviews with Baldwin by the U.S. Naval Institute at Annapolis, Maryland. Because of the profound influence the *Times* exerts on all of the rest of American journalism,[2] in particular the networks and the weekly news magazines, the internal *New York Times* dispute over Vietnam coverage lies at the core of the lasting hostility and distrust between the military and the press that is the long-term legacy of the Vietnam War.

The defining moment both in Baldwin's defeat within the corporate structure of the *Times* and in the likely permanent embitterment embodied in the relationship between the press and the U.S. military was the visit by Harrison E. Salisbury, then an assistant managing editor of the *Times*, to North Vietnam in December 1966. At that time U.S. forces were engaged in combat with North Vietnam in defense of South Vietnam.

During a U.S. Naval Institute oral history interview, Baldwin charged that Salisbury "wasn't in Vietnam more than 24 hours before he filed his first story. It contained almost verbatim . . . a release which the North Vietnamese had been pedaling all over Europe for several months and had found nobody would take it, charging the United States with bombing the dikes and deliberately trying to flood their country. He incorporated this in his first story without any attribution to Hanoi."

"It struck me then—and it still does," Baldwin wrote many years later, "that it was damn near treasonable to send a correspondent to Hanoi and to print in the paper the information he gathered (with the connivance and assistance of the enemy), without labeling it as coming from enemy sources, some of [it] absurdly inaccurate (. . . a small piece of metal Salisbury was shown he identified—I certainly couldn't have done it—as part of an American bomb . . .)."[3]

Baldwin had not been informed of the Salisbury trip, nor was he given the opportunity to read the reports from Hanoi prior to publication, although they dealt with matters clearly within the purview of a military editor. Immediately upon appearance of the first article, Baldwin wrote a memorandum to Clifton Daniel, then managing editor, warning that the Salisbury reporting "seems to put Mr. Salisbury and the *Times* squarely on the side of North Vietnam . . . [T]he final paragraph implies that we are deliberately and consistently bombing civilian targets. As you know, I have been foremost in criticizing what I considered to be the deception and untruths emanating from the Pentagon and elsewhere in Washington not only about the Vietnam war but about other subjects but I do not think it is fair or accurate to make judgements based on statistics from Communist sources and print them as gospel without some qualification. . . . "[4]

In response to these and other criticisms of the Salisbury reporting, Daniel replied, "I agree with you that some of Harrison's material has not been properly attributed. . . . We have already asked him to be careful about this." Baldwin's memorandum, Daniel said, "provides the basis for a very much needed story. I hope it can be couched in terms attributing it to the military and other Washington sources so that we will not give the appearance of presenting an argument between two members of our own staff."[5]

Baldwin obediently wrote a "Pentagon-sources" story which appeared the next day. He found it a "very awkward, strange way of doing business for a great newspaper."[6]

There was no question in Baldwin's mind that Salisbury's instantaneous transmission of North Vietnamese propaganda claims without attribution was a quid pro quo for having been granted access to North Vietnam, engineered, in Baldwin's view, through Wilfrid Burchett, an Australian Communist journalist.[7]

As Mike Wallace of CBSs News's "60 Minutes" would agree many years later, the Salisbury visit to North Vietnam was "only one step away" from the horrific hypothetical situation presented during Columbia University journalism ethics seminars in which American journalists accompanying an enemy patrol find themselves about to be witness to the ambush of Americans.

To the U.S. military, the Salisbury reporting was nothing less than treason, on a par with actress Jane Fonda's posing with a North Vietnamese anti-aircraft crew preparing to fire on American aircraft.[8] The lasting distrust for the press thus engendered on the part of many, if not most, U.S. officers of all services has been described by everyone who has encountered it, shorn of the pretenses necessary to maintain a workable day-to-day relationship, as "hatred." The reaction of the Marine colonel, described in Chapter 3, during the Columbia ethics seminars to what Wallace recognized as a hypothetical situation closely linked to the Salisbury reporting during the Vietnam War and to reporting by CNN's Peter Arnett from Baghdad during the Persian Gulf War is a rare, but portentous, public expression of that bitterness.

As Baldwin stated in his memorandum to Clifton Daniel, he had "been foremost in criticizing . . . deception and untruths emanating from the Pentagon. . . . " But he was in at least as much trouble for that at the *Times* as he would be for having challenged the decision of the *Times*'s top management to send Salisbury to North Vietnam and to publish as fact Salisbury's unverified transmission of North Vietnamese propaganda claims.

In retrospect, Baldwin traced all of that to an attitudinal change in the top management of the *Times* following the death of Arthur Hays Sulzberger.

"I think it was noticeable when [A. H. Sulzberger] died that the influence at the *Times*, which was sympathetic to a sound and very strong defense, became less pronounced at high levels. . . . [A. O. "Punch" Sulzberger, son and successor, in 1963, to A. H. Sulzberger] proved to be, from an economic and business point of view, an extremely able publisher, not equally able, I think, from the point of view of the contents of the paper. . . . 'Punch' is also extremely influenced . . . by the liberal circles he's moved in in New York and by his second wife."[9]

This was reinforced, Baldwin believed, by "the accession to [control of] the editorial page of John Oakes [another member of the publisher's family] who's a very liberal, fine person, but had a kind of do-gooder, sophomoric attitude without much . . . comprehension in certain fields. Whether it was his doing or whether it was the publisher's doing, or whether it was a mutual interaction between them, the *Times* quickly reflected what I thought was an anti-Vietnam bias, and, increasingly, a kind of anti-military bias."[10]

In 1965, for the first time in a history that included two world wars and the Korean War, the *Times* omitted a Christmas greeting to U.S. forces in combat.

That the *Times* top management had become increasingly hostile to the Vietnam War effort was reflected in its sponsorship of the unprecedented Salisbury visit to an enemy nation in time of war. At the same time that management became the ardent political supporter of President John F. Kennedy and of the civilian administration that Kennedy had installed in the Pentagon in 1961, and that remained in place under President Lyndon B. Johnson.

As Baldwin noted in his memorandum to Managing Editor Clifton Daniel criticizing the Salisbury reporting, Baldwin had been challenging the "deception and untruths" of the Kennedy-Johnson Pentagon management concerning other than Vietnam for many months. Yet it was precisely that challenge to people closely connected with and greatly admired by the new, strongly liberal *Times* management that had so greatly undermined Baldwin's influence. As a result, he would learn of the Salisbury trip to North Vietnam only shortly before he read the initial dispatch in the paper.

To the strong liberal, pro-Kennedy political attachment, in Baldwin's view, there was added a strong affinity on the part of A. O. Sulzberger to the management philosophy of the Pentagon's new civilian chiefs, led by Secretary of Defense Robert S. McNamara, former chief executive of the Ford Motor Company. The heart and soul of this philosophy was a belief that all problems could be reduced to numbers—"quantification"—by means of mathematical "systems analysis." That put the McNamara regime at loggerheads with a military leadership who believed that the human equation in war, not the statistics, is paramount.

With many other journalists, Baldwin had been appalled by the assertion following the Cuban missile crisis of 1962 by McNamara's public relations chief, Arthur Sylvester, that the government has a "right to lie."[11]

Before Vietnam there was TFX (Tactical Fighter Experimental). For Baldwin and a few other long-term specialists in military reporting the TFX controversy would demonstrate that the "right to lie" was accepted by the Kennedy administration, in particular by its appointees in the Pentagon, as a routine way of doing business.

McNamara took office as secretary of defense at the end of fourteen years of intense, often bitter public debate within and among the armed forces over post–World War II roles and missions. Although that debate often centered on particular weapons systems (bombers, aircraft carriers, missiles), much more profound issues of national strategy, even of national morality, were involved. Generally, the press regarded the debates as an annoyance. As early as 1949, for example, the then *Washington Daily News* would greet appointment of a new deputy defense secretary with the headline "Steve Early's Job Is to Muzzle the Loud-Mouth Brass in Pentagon."[12] It is an odd attitude for a medium that claims to be a vital forum for discussion of public issues.

Although then Senator John F. Kennedy had used one such issue, a supposed "missile gap" portrayed by the Air Force as a growing Soviet advantage over the United States, in his campaign for the presidency, McNamara moved quickly upon taking office to shut off all such public controversy.

As a candidate, Kennedy had also been influenced by people, among them

Henry Kissinger and former Army Chief of Staff Maxwell Taylor, who touted
the then nascent Army Special Forces ("Green Berets") as the means of
dealing with Third World conflicts, such as that left over from the French
colonial regime in Vietnam, without committing large conventional military
forces.[13] When George Decker, then Army chief of staff, warned that there
was no such panacea and that military involvement at any level would lead
to a major war, he was promptly fired. The press exulted. At last, ran the
universal editorial theme, "heads were being knocked together."

Similar hosannas followed the firing, in 1963, of Admiral George W. Anderson as chief of naval operations after Anderson objected to McNamara's
giving orders to specific ships during the 1962 Cuban missile crisis. The
process was now in place by which every aircraft sortie over North Vietnam
in coming years would be determined solely by civilians on Tuesday of each
week at a White House luncheon.[14]

During the same period McNamara moved to consolidate the previously
quasi-independent military service public relations operations under a single, all-powerful civilian assistant secretary of defense for public affairs, the
same Arthur Sylvester who would proclaim a "right to lie." No longer would
it be possible for a reporter to go from one service public affairs office to
the next and obtain varying opinions about weapons systems, strategy, and
the like. All now would "sing out of the same book," or else.

So some two years passed before the press began to discover the significance of a note in the first Kennedy defense budget that $45 million had
been set aside for development of a four-service fighter-interceptor with a
then innovative variable wing sweep. As Professor Robert J. Art of Brandeis
University and a Senate investigating committee would establish a decade
later, that decision "to develop one plane, and one plane only, which would
fulfill the tactical fighter needs of all military branches—Air Force, Navy,
Marine Corps, and Army" was made in February 1961, less than a month
after the Kennedy administration took office, not through scientific or quasi-
scientific "systems analysis," but solely on the basis of a hunch, by Mc-
Namara, that it would be a good idea.[15]

The Air Force and Navy opposed the "'commonality" idea from the beginning and until late in 1962 succeeded in maintaining parallel development
programs. Those would have led to separate aircraft configured to divergent,
indeed, contradictory, Air Force and Navy needs.

Overruling the military, McNamara opted for the program that promised
to conform to his commonality objective. When General Accounting Office
auditors later inquired as to the basis of that decision, McNamara replied
that he "made a rough judgment from his experience as an official at Ford."[16]
General Decker and Admiral Anderson had been fired, actions receiving
fulsome praise from the nation's editorial writers, for having opposed
McNamara with just such "rough judgments" based, unlike McNamara's,
on a lifetime of military experience and training.

"The major issue that troubles many in the service," Hanson Baldwin of the *Times* wrote in a commentary published on March 2, 1963, "is that a tremendous contract has been awarded purely on the basis of brochures . . . before a single plane has flown." This was made possible, he said, by "the tremendous centralization of authority in all fields within the office of the Secretary. Neither industry nor the services believed the differing requirements of planes intended to provide air superiority, close air support, reconnaissance and [long-range] interdiction and capable of operating from short forward fields or carrier decks could possibly be combined in one plane without major sacrifice of the combat requirements."

This is the one and only warning the public would get of a disaster that would consume some $10 billion, in 1960s money, and finally produce an aircraft (F–111, FB–111) that could be used only from 10,000-foot land runways for two missions, interdiction and medium-range bombardment. A senatorial investigation early in 1963 seeking to explore such criticisms as Baldwin had surfaced had been overwhelmed by press support for McNamara.

Building on an adulatory report by its respected Washington correspondent, Richard L. Strout, the *Christian Science Monitor* declared, "Nothing has been said . . . to shake faith in the judgment and competence of Mr. McNamara. . . . We trust he will continue to make the big and difficult decisions. . . ."[17]

Walter Lippmann, then the premier international columnist, acknowledged in the *Washington Post* that "after swimming around . . . in the sea of technical detail of the TFX argument . . . I emerged wondering, since there is so much that I do not understand, whether there is anything which I am entitled to write about." That did not stop him from concluding that "In Secretary McNamara the country has a Secretary of Defense who in his training, in his practical experience, and in his technical knowledge of production, is remarkably, perhaps uniquely, qualified to pass judgment on a problem like that of the TFX."[18]

The *Philadelphia Inquirer* addressed itself directly to the senators who were questioning Mr. McNamara's judgment: "Congressional critics . . . should avoid tactics which seem to border on harassment of an exceptionally well-qualified public official."[19]

Within the *New York Times* itself, Hanson Baldwin's cautionary words were indirectly rebuked by James Reston, Washington bureau chief, close confidant of the new *Times* management, and close friend and ardent admirer of the Kennedys. "Secretary of Defense McNamara is gradually managing to make his policies prevail at the Pentagon," Reston wrote, "but there is still an ugly fight ahead. . . . He is often challenging the military judgment of the senior officers. . . . When Elihu Root established the General Staff of the Army under President McKinley . . . he encountered very much the same opposition to change."[20]

The pursuit of commonality was now unstoppable.

Along the way, in 1965, two admirals objected to McNamara judgments concerning retention of Navy shipyards. The *Denver Post* suggested "the resignations be duly and promptly accepted," solely on faith in Mr. McNamara's judgment.[21]

Also in 1965 the United States plunged massively into the Vietnam War.

"In many ways the war in Viet Nam really is 'McNamara's war,'" Richard Fryklund, Pentagon correspondent of the *Washington Star*, commented. "He has done more to shape that conflict than anyone outside the Viet Cong. . . . First of all, take present policies. To a large extent they are McNamara's, adopted during his first year in office [and] accepted by President Kennedy. . . . It was McNamara who took the principle of civilian control [beyond what any of his predecessors had done]. . . . The result is civilians are in complete control of the war in Viet Nam. They dictate strategy, and closely supervise tactics. The basic strategy has been slow escalation of bombing in the north and counter-guerrilla operations, shading into conventional war, in the south. Escalation is a McNamara device which makes military men uncomfortable. If [the military chiefs] had their way . . . they either would not be bombing at all or they long ago would have destroyed North Viet Nam."[22]

Warnings from Hanson Baldwin that the military chiefs were telling McNamara his strategy would require 1 million men and "many years" of struggle either went unheeded or never made it into print as Baldwin encountered increasing opposition from pro-McNamara editors at every level of *New York Times* management.[23]

The chorus of press support continued well into 1966. "Robert McNamara has turned out to be President Johnson's strong right arm," the *Houston Chronicle* declared. "He is by almost everybody's appraisal one of the most competent cabinet members Washington has seen in many a year and is probably the best Defense secretary ever."[24]

By March 1970, the extent of what the *Louisville Courier-Journal* would describe as "the F–111 boondoggle" could no longer be concealed.[25]

As early as 1967, Bernard D. Nossiter of the *Washington Post* would report that McNamara was "plaintively" asking where responsibility for recurrent engine problems lay. "Air Force Secretary Harold Brown said we don't know." Basically, the problem lay with the contradictory weight, landing speed, and configuration requirements dictated by the demand for commonality. Twenty-three pages of a senatorial investigation, Nossiter reported, "offer a rare glimpse of powerful officials desperately trying to cope with a multibillion-dollar procurement fiasco, a suspicious press and a relentless investigating senator [Sen. John L. McClellan]."[26]

A suspicious press? Except for Baldwin's lone voice, not until the damage to the public interest was irrevocable.

Other than Baldwin of the *Times*, only one newsman, Clark R. Mollenhoff,

Washington correspondent of the *Minneapolis Tribune*, had eventually challenged McNamara's judgment in regard to the TFX in time to avoid at least some of the enormous fiscal damage.[27]

Mollenhoff attributed the failure to stop the wrongheaded drive for commonality, to "lack of diligence on the part of the press. . . . [R]eporters and columnists failed in their role as watchdogs because they did not know their subject. . . . There were only about a dozen reporters who read the whole record of the [1963] investigation. . . . However, there were dozens of apologists for McNamara. . . . They have written from Pentagon handouts and from 'confidential' inside information straight from [McNamara]."

The press had created a demigod, and he had failed.

Meanwhile, what of "McNamara's war" in Vietnam? The Henry Kissinger–Maxwell Taylor idea of disposing of such as the Vietnam problem by sending over a few Special Forces detachments had not worked. The Special Forces were designed for a very particular situation in Europe: If war broke out there with the Soviet Union, specially trained teams with appropriate language qualifications would be parachuted behind Soviet lines to organize resistance by Poles, Hungarians, East Germans, and other dissident populations. To that end, Americans of those nationalities who still spoke their ancestral languages and refugees from such as the Hungarian Revolution of 1956 had been intensively recruited.

Special Forces detachments would perform heroic service on the perimeter of allied forces in Vietnam where they succeeded, in spite of the cultural barriers, in organizing tribes native to the border regions against the North Vietnamese. But they were largely irrelevant to the steadily increasing military pressure North Vietnam was building against South Vietnam.

Just as General George Decker, the Army chief of staff fired early in the Kennedy administration, had warned, commitment of U.S. forces, in particular land forces, to Vietnam would lead inevitably to a massive requirement. The Kennedy administration was caught up very quickly in a web of its own making.

When it became apparent that a few handfuls of Green Berets were not going to resolve the problem, McNamara's doctrine of "escalation" came into force.

First, advisers were drawn from the mainline U.S. Army units General Decker had warned would inevitably become involved and were deployed to South Vietnamese army units. With only the rarest exceptions, the U.S. advisers knew little or nothing of Asian history and culture, let alone of the highly specialized history and culture of Vietnam. They seldom stayed long enough to become proficient in the language. Worse, often when a South Vietnamese unit was trapped, helicopters came to lift the Americans out of danger, leaving the Vietnamese to their fate.

But with the can-do attitude bred of their largely North American and European service, the advisers set about converting what was essentially a leftover French colonial army into a modern fighting force. That pitted them against the cultural forces of family and locality and the age-old patterns of corruption that the Americans neither understood nor were prepared to tolerate.

Enter now a group of news reporters who were at least as ignorant of the basic elements of the struggle as was the great majority of the U.S. advisers.

David Halberstam, then of the *New York Times*, was twenty-seven, a general assignment reporter on various U.S. newspapers who had been sent by the *Times* to cover United Nations peacekeeping operations in the Congo and from there to cover Vietnam. He acknowledges that his total acquaintance with military operations of any sort had consisted of "one session [in the Congo] with live machine guns and a visit to a field hospital." His orientation on Vietnam consisted of a few books read en route and a talk with a *Times* Asian correspondent in Hong Kong.[28]

Peter Arnett, a New Zealand citizen employed by the AP, recalls that his orientation on Asia consisted of listening "with glee and disbelief to . . . ribald tales of the Shanghai whorehouses in the closing days of [the Chinese Civil] war."[29]

Neil Sheehan, then of UPI, graduated from Harvard in 1959 and had spent two years in the Army, most of it as a writer for *Pacific Stars and Stripes* in Tokyo.

As would be confirmed many years later in Sheehan's book *A Bright Shining Lie*, these three, the core of the U.S. news operation in Vietnam during the crucial years from 1961 to 1963, came under the influence of a mid-level U.S. Army adviser, Lieutenant Colonel John Paul Vann, who was convinced that he had solved the riddle of how to galvanize what was essentially a fifteenth-century South Vietnamese army into a twentieth-century fighting force: Get rid of South Vietnamese President Ngo Dinh Diem, and have the United States take over the war, in toto.

Here was the unavoidable intersection of military and political reporting that Hanson Baldwin cited in the U.S. Naval Institute interviews, with equally unavoidable questions concerning the competence of those entrusted with such reporting and of their supervisors. Here also arose an issue that American journalism is still seeking to avoid: Does the work of the journalist, ipso facto, make the journalist a participant in and a shaper of the events he or she is writing about?

President Diem had impeccable Vietnamese nationalist credentials, having opposed French colonial rule throughout his adult life and having been jailed for it. He had taken office through the only democratic election any part of the country had known in its history. Like several million Vietnamese, he was a Roman Catholic. He was also a man of his own culture, deeply enmeshed in the family and geographic loyalties that the U.S. advisers, the Vann group in particular, found intolerable.

The man in the middle of it all was U.S. Army General Paul D. Harkins, chief of the U.S. military advisory group. Harkins did not consider the overthrowing of a legitimately elected head of state to be among his options. Indeed, the history of the period that came to light several years later with the publication of the so-called "Pentagon Papers" would show that the entire U.S. military command structure regarded such involvements as abhorrent, virtually the repudiation of the U.S. military ethic. That had been defined originally by General George Washington and reaffirmed during the Civil War when Union General George B. McClellan hinted at the idea of a coup and was told by his staff and subordinate commanders in no uncertain terms that the Army of the Potomac would not follow him and, indeed, would probably arrest him.

Vann launched what, in effect, was a mutiny, using his young and impressionable news reporters as the lever with which to subvert Harkins's policy of working within the Diem regime and, ultimately, to depose Diem. Central to this campaign was Vann's expert exploitation of what was made to appear to be a South Vietnamese debacle at Ap Bac in January 1963.

As described by a participant, Colonel Andrew P. O'Meara, Jr.,[30] "The battle had been initiated as a result of a rather ambitious tactical operation that saw a link-up between airmobile and mechanized troops. . . . The airmobile troops found themselves on a hot [defended] landing zone. The link-up was unsuccessful. Heavy losses were sustained in the airmobile assault. . . . The [South Vietnamese] tactical employment of the mechanized unit was intially quite aggressive. Once they recognized that they were faced by a serious obstacle [a canal] covered by fire they initially laid down a base of fire and attempted to assault. The marksmanship of the Viet Cong riflemen was excellent. Most of the [South Vietnamese] 50 caliber gunners died of head wounds within the opening minutes of the fight. In some cases, two or three men had died in succession at those guns. . . . "

The principal element in the failure to trap a large Viet Cong force, in O'Meara's view, was one of intelligence, in that the airmobile unit attempted to insert on a defended drop zone. The intelligence on which the South Vietnamese were operating had been furnished entirely by Americans, according to O'Meara, "based on radio intercept."

Back at the division headquarters, O'Meara observed Lieutenant Colonel Vann "spilling his gut to the press. . . . I observed [him] talking to Halberstam of the *New York Times*. . . . Vann was red in the face and loudly denouncing the [South Vietnamese] for cowardice and incompetence."

Based on Vann's polemic, Halberstam reported the Ap Bac fight entirely in those terms. No mention was made of the inadequate and misleading U.S. intelligence or of the heroism of South Vietnamese soldiers who moved to those 50 caliber machine guns knowing they faced certain death. Although O'Meara was a visible and obvious source, no attempt was made to interview him. In this and other instances, Sheehan and Arnett followed Halberstam's guidance from Vann almost word for word.

In the streets of Saigon and other South Vietnamese cities another drama was occurring. Buddhist bonzes [priests] who had never before been a factor in Vietnamese politics and who would never appear thereafter began representing themselves as spokesmen for a Buddhist "majority" being persecuted by the Roman Catholic Diem. To focus attention on their cause individual priests and Buddhist nuns periodically set themselves aflame. In each case the Saigon press corps was notified in advance of the time and place of the immolation. In several cases reporters could have intervened to save the life of the victim, but chose not to do so.

Halberstam, Sheehan, and Arnett responded to the Buddhist activists exactly as they had to Vann and his true believers among the advisers. Horrific pictures of the immolations appeared on every front page in the United States, first and foremost on that of the *New York Times*. In the accompanying stories, Halberstam never failed to identify the South Vietnamese president as the "Roman Catholic Diem." Never before or since has the *Times* or any other reputable American newspaper so relentlessly identified a public figure, American or foreign, by religion.

In all this, Halberstam, Sheehan, and Arnett encountered a formidable opponent.

Marguerite Higgins was born in Hong Kong of a family with deep roots in Asia. She had become a combat correspondent in World War II and had won a Pulitzer Prize for her battlefield reporting during the Korean War. She had served as Tokyo bureau chief for the *New York Herald-Tribune* and had visited Vietnam on six occasions before the U.S. phase of the war began.

Higgins traveled throughout South Vietnam during the period in which the anti-Diem campaign sponsored by Vann in the battle areas and by the Buddhist activists in the cities was at its height. In articles in the *Herald-Tribune* and later in a book[31] and magazine articles she condemned the anti-Diem reporting. Her principal conclusions were these:

- That the anti-Diem Buddhist campaign was politically rather than religiously motivated and was confined to a small group of urban militants.
- That the Buddhist campaign had no relevance to the concerns of the majority of the Vietnamese population who were neither Buddhist nor Catholics, but Taoists.
- That the suicides by fire, and a heavily reported demonstration in the city of Hue, far from being the spontaneous actions of "persecuted" victims, were carefully planned and staged media events to exploit the appetite of the American press for sensational stories and pictures.
- That, whatever the defects of the Diem regime, the likely replacements could only be worse.[32]

Higgins also challenged the unrelievedly pessimistic assessment of the South Vietnamese army performance being transmitted by Vann and like-minded advisers through their press contacts. In this she was supported by reporters who accompanied South Vietnamese units more regularly than did Halberstam and the other Saigon correspondents—principally Keyes Beech,[33] for many years Asian correspondent for the *Chicago Daily News*, and Jim G. Lucas of the Scripps-Howard newspapers, both with extensive experience in military coverage dating to World War II.

As the wife of a U.S. Air Force general, Higgins was regarded by the greater part of the American press as suspect, doubly so because of her French and Irish background which led to her being identified as a Catholic in stories seeking to counterbalance her criticism of Halberstam and the wire service reporters. She was not a Catholic.

Despite her credentials, journalistic, cultural, and military, Higgins could not successfully oppose the *New York Times*.

In the aftermath of the Oliver Stone movie, *JFK*, in 1991 public discussion as to whether President John F. Kennedy would have sustained and expanded the U.S. effort in Vietnam, had he not been assassinated in November 1963, was renewed.[34]

At the very least, the exchange of published statements by Kennedy advisers documents an ambivalence. Public statements indicate a determination to press on, and private statements indicate a more mixed—indeed, vacillating—attitude entirely consistent with his performance during the Bay of Pigs incident in 1961 and later when the Berlin Wall was emplaced. All that can be said with any certainty is that Kennedy, powerfully influenced by what he was reading every day in the *New York Times*, acceded to a request by Roger Hilsman, assistant secretary of state for Asian affairs, that U.S. backing be given to South Vietnamese military figures who were plotting to overthrow President Diem.

President Diem was overthrown and murdered in November 1963, the same month in which Kennedy would meet his death. If, indeed, Kennedy had intended to extricate the United States from Vietnam, nothing could have been more in opposition to that objective than becoming involved in a *coup d'état* by which the United States became identified with and obligated to support the successor regime it had sponsored.

The sum of Marguerite Higgins's argument was whether Diem was better than chaos. What was done, in her view, was to turn a Vietnamese war into an American war, with a likely outcome that filled her with dread. Her papers, at Syracuse University, show a deepening shadow.

Increasingly denied a forum in a press that had by now very nearly canonized the assassinated U.S. president, she tried so much the harder to pit her diminishing strength against the disaster that she still hoped might be avoidable. Against the advice of editors, family, and friends she returned to Vietnam again and again, each time incurring ailments plainly related to a growing exhaustion. She died at Walter Reed Army Medical Center in Washington in January 1966, shortly after her tenth visit to Vietnam. Among her papers at Syracuse is a clipping of a story "buried" deep within the *New*

York Times under the *Times*'s smallest headline type. It reported the suicide by fire of a seventeen-year-old Vietnamese girl. It is dated December 1, 1963, three weeks after Diem's murder.

If John F. Kennedy had been vacillating about his commitment to South Vietnam, Halberstam and Sheehan were every bit as demanding of a total U.S. involvement as was their mentor, John Paul Vann.

"What *about* withdrawal?" Halberstam would ask months later in his book *The Making of a Quagmire*. "Few Americans who have served in Vietnam can stomach this idea. . . . Withdrawal [would] mean the United States' prestige would be lowered throughout the world. . . . The lesson to be learned from Vietnam is that we must get in earlier. . . . "[35]

Sheehan was very quickly rewarded with a job on the *Times*, yet so deep was his own continuing commitment to Vann's political and military objectives that he made sure his sentiments were known to the *Times*'s one and only believer in a possible US. victory. Thus, in a letter to Hanson Baldwin, Sheehan declared his belief that "we are accomplishing something in Vietnam. . . . We are beginning to employ our military power . . . effectively. Military power is all we really can apply to Vietnam, but we have so much of it that through its sheer weight w may be able to prevail in the end."[36]

A quarter of a century later, to judge by his book *A Bright Shining Lie*, Sheehan still had not learned what the more politically astute Marguerite Higgins had understood in an instant: that military power cannot survive the collapse of its political base. Whatever its flaws, the Diem regime was the only legitimate base the United States ever possessed in Vietnam.

Political chaos, never to be resolved, was, as Higgins had warned, the lasting and fatal legacy of the anti-Diem coup. A legitimately elected head of state with demonstrated Vietnamese nationalist credentials had been replaced by former French colonial non-commissioned officers, vaulted by the U.S. State Department and the president it served into the presidential palace in what one U.S. observer, U.S. Army Colonel Thomas A. Ware, would describe as "the bum-of-the-week regimes."

Were Halberstam, Sheehan, and Arnett and their supervisors in New York mere recorders of this decline into chaos and, therefore, without any degree of accountability or blame for the results? Or were they participants? If participants, what was the basis for the profound judgments they made as to who would rule in South Vietnam, who would live or die? There was no doubt in the minds of General Harkins and many other senior U.S. officers. They would hold the press personally and institutionally responsible both for the murder of Diem and for all that followed.[37]

The overarching strategic limit prescribed in Washington for "McNamara's war" was that nothing was to be done that might provoke a larger war with China or the Soviet Union, notably an invasion of North Vietnam. The assumptions underlying that limit had operated in 1962 during the Cuban missile crisis when the Kennedy administration led the public to believe that the Soviet Union was ready to risk the Russian homeland to preserve the likes of Fidel Castro. As it turned out, once a decision was finally made, too late, to mine the principal North Vietnamese port through which Russian war materiel flowed, the Soviets simply stayed away.

The operational doctrine by which the Vietnam War was to be fought within this mistaken strategic context was, as Richard Fryklund of the *Washington Star* had described it, "escalation," the product of over a decade of academic analysis and criticism of Allied objectives in World War II, by which such terms as "unconditional surrender" and "victory" became what would later be called "politically incorrect." At some point, Robert Mc-Namara's systems analysts calculated, North Vietnam would have no choice but to accede to the logic of a certain number of casualties, a certain number of bombs dropped, and so on. Hence, the notorious emphasis throughout the U.S. phase of the war on body counts. The chief McNamara systems analyst, Alain Enthoven, and many other Kennedy Pentagon appointees, had arrived on the scene in Washington in 1961, innocent of military service and proclaiming that military history had begun all over again at ground zero with the first nuclear explosion in 1945. This group of officials was dubbed and routinely reported by a worshipful press as "the whiz kids."

North Vietnam and its sponsors also could practice "escalation." Their exploitation of the chaos that followed President Diem's overthrow and the unholy alliance that this had produced between the United States and his murderers dictated, in early 1965, the massive intervention by mainline U.S. combat forces that General Decker had warned would be the likely consequence of the adviser effort.

The dismissals of General Decker and Admiral Anderson had virtually silenced any further military demurrers to the McNamara-Enthoven theses of war. Even so, General Harold K. Johnson, General Decker's successor as Army chief of staff, warned when the large-scale intervention began that it would take a million men and at least ten years to defeat North Vietnam within the restrictions the McNamara regime had imposed, by now with the acquiescence of President Johnson.[38]

Yet so supportive was the press of the McNamara team's contempt for traditional military judgment that General Johnson's warning was scarcely reported,[39] as was the case with the earlier warnings from high military sources Hanson Baldwin attempted to transmit. Just as the greater part of American journalism supported McNamara until disaster could no longer be concealed in the TFX affair, often with clearly expressed contempt for the military leadership, so it had given him something very near adulation up to the point where the United States was so deeply committed to an impossible political situation in Vietnam that the disaster Marguerite Higgins had worked herself to death to try to avert could no longer be avoided or ignored.

When the disaster was finally recognized, it was neither McNamara and his "whiz kids" nor the academic fathers of escalation who would be blamed. The blame would fall, first and foremost, on Lyndon Johnson.

As vice president, Johnson had opposed U.S. involvement in the overthrow of Diem. But, mesmerized by the presumed wizardries of the Pentagon regime he inherited as president and keenly aware of the enormous support they enjoyed in the press, he made the fatal mistake of keeping them on. And the blame would fall, not least of all, on the military, to the extent that veterans returning from the combat theater would be spat on in airport lounges by draft-deferred students at the instigation of teachers from the same faculties that had spawned escalation. Many of those teachers had been deferred themselves from the Korean War draft.

It was print and wire service journalism—personified by Halberstam, Sheehan, and Arnett in Vietnam and a host of McNamara-worshiping editorial writers in the United States—who had sowed hatred for the press among the higher ranks of the military. It would be television that brought those seeds to an evil germination not only in the top ranks, but also throughout the military, to include veterans of all ranks who would carry a message of distrust and hatred to their civilian homes and families.

As every careful survey on the subject has shown, no other part of American journalism so visibly, literally, takes its moral and political guidance from the *New York Times* as does network television. In general, it is the only newspaper—indeed, generally the only print document of any length— that national television anchors, correspondents, and producers have time to read. Any viewer can verify that for himself or herself simply by reading the *Times* closely, day by day for at least a year, and watching the frequency with which *Times* news items, in particular feature stories, appear on the network news broadcast twenty-four to forty-eight hours, or more, later, often scarcely rewritten, but without attribution to the newspaper.

Before the large-scale U.S. intervention in 1965, television covered Vietnam only sporadically, mainly from bureaus in Tokyo and Hong Kong. The infusion of major U.S. units made the war a "hometown" story all across the country. The networks established full-time bureaus in Saigon, and its correspondents fought for the assignment. With rare exceptions, those correspondents were even more innocent of military and Asian, let alone Vietnamese, backgrounds than was the case with the print and wire service reporters who played so major a role in the overthrow of President Diem. And they left New York deeply ingrained with the growing anti-Vietnam, anti-military viewpoint of the *Times* editors who had supported from New York the Halberstam and Vann campaign against Diem.

Baldwin was the first to notice and to record that the new policies were not confined to editorials. "The *Times* changed completely. . . . Editorial policy in the thirties could be described in two words to be against sin, to be against Hitler, and nothing else. . . . Their editorials were bland, often quite well written, on a great many different subjects, but we didn't take any very strong stands. And that was a deliberate policy of Adolph Ochs [the founder]. He didn't believe that a paper could take a strong editorial stand and still preserve objective news columns. He thought that the tail would wag the dog, and I think that has happened."[40]

The extent to which this was true was confirmed many years later when a *Times* reporter dared to challenge editorial positions that related to the most sensitive of all possible issues at the paper, the close social relationship between the newspaper's founding family and the British royal family. "Punch" Sulzberger himself took a personal role in forcing her out of her job when she refused, in a luncheon with Sulzberger, to conform her reporting to the editorials.[41]

Within the *Times* itself the unprecedented latitude given Halberstam had long since made it obvious that the path to journalistic glory lay in providing news-column support for the *Times*'s editorial positions and prejudices.

"I was appalled by the bias I found in the *Times* reporters,"[42] Baldwin said of his first visit to Vietnam in 1965. During his second visit, in 1967, he encountered "a wild man, a very fine writer, but a wild man, not the sort of person emotionally who should have been covering Vietnam."[43] Baldwin later identified the "wild man" as Robert Kleiman.[44] By the latter stages of the Vietnam War, Kleiman was a principal author of the *Times* editorials on all defense subjects.[45] Baldwin held Kleiman responsible for destroying the *Times* military research capability built up over the previous three decades and for forcing into retirement the *Times*'s last professional military research specialist.

If the television news correspondents had not fully absorbed the *Times*'s view of the war by the time they got to Vietnam, they were sometimes more forcibly instructed.

Liz Trotta, then of NBC, newly arrived in Vietnam, witnessed an incident when, during a private dinner party, another American correspondent "dared voice support for the war." "Charlie Mohr of the *Times*," Trotta recalled, "lunged over the roasted chicken, grabbed [the man who "dared voice support"] by his shirt front, and threatened to rearrange his face."[46]

A television correspondent who ran counter to what the New York network executives were reading in the *Times* would face much worse consequences. He or she would simply be professionally smothered. "Politically correct" was a way of life in national American journalism long before it became famous on the academic campus. An atmosphere and a mindset had been created in New York, while the war-correspondents-to-be were still shopping for their safari suits, that would be understood to justify any form of reporting so long as the ultimate anti-war message was conveyed.

The wounds inflicted by this process of induced bias were many and deep.

On October 9, 1967, "CBS Evening News" broadcast film showing a U.S. soldier attempting to cut off the ear of a dead enemy soldier. The Army immediately brought charges against the soldier, such conduct being in

violation of the Rules of Land Warfare, of which the United Stats is a sig-
natory. Those rules are implemented in the U.S. Uniform Code of Military
Justice on the provisions on which all U.S. soldiers are instructed during
basic training. During the trial it developed that the soldier had been urged
on by CBS reporters Don Webster and John Smith, Smith having supplied
the knife. The soldier was convicted. Smith and Webster were not charged.

Two years later, still employed by CBS, Webster figured in another incident, broadcast on November 3, 1969, which appeared to portray the
stabbing of a captured enemy soldier by a South Vietnamese in the presence
of U.S. personnel. The U.S. embassy in Saigon presented convincing evidence that the report had been put together using film clips from different
locales, U.S. training films, and varying personnel to produce the desired,
and fictitious, effect. CBS refused to assist in the investigation of the incident,
but did not challenge the embassy report.

In early February 1968, U.S. Army Colonel Ronald A. Roberge, then
senior province adviser at Vinh Long, was asked the following questions by
a network television crew, concerning the then recent Communist Tet offensive:

Q: Did you receive any warning from [U.S. military headquarters] of the Tet attack?

A: Yes, as we had many times in the past. We anticipated attacks in the district, but
we did not anticipate an attack on Vinh Long itself.

Q: Did the Vietnamese have any idea such an attack was coming?

A: Hell no! Or if they did they didn't tell me.[47]

Friends of Roberge told him later that the interview as broadcast had been
edited to make the answer to the second question appear to be the answer
to the first question, the question of advance warning by senior U.S. headquarters having become an important political issue at home.

As was the case with the expertly distorted 1969 Webster stabbing report,
that editing was done in New York, in an atmosphere described by Professor
John Roche of Brandeis University who, while serving as an adviser to
President Johnson, was called on frequently to appear on network news
"shows." "At the junior producer level," Professor Roche told future television news host John McLaughlin, "there are a lot of very bright college-
educated guys, still in their twenties who decide which film clips to run.
Just before going on the air, staffers would ask me how anyone can support
an immoral war. The producer was using a picture of Johnson for a dart-
board."[48]

As Roche's experience indicates, the emotional bias may have been more
extreme at CBS than at the other networks, but it prevailed throughout.
Virtually every U.S. officer of whatever rank who served in Vietnam, and
many enlisted persons as well, who had contact with television news crews
reported incidents, if not of deliberate fakery, of ignorance, ineptitude, and

an obsession with action-packed photography to the exclusion of all else.[49] Threaded through it all was the bias reflected by those young producers in New York, imbibed from nowhere else than the editorials and ideologically infected news columns of the *New York Times*, the only comprehensive report of the war to which those producers and the more senior executives had ever been exposed.

There were rare exceptions to the general atmosphere of messianism and irresponsibility. Bill Wordham of ABC News was eyewitness to repeated incidents in which Marines had died because their M–16 rifles had jammed. Although the Marine chain of command bitterly and vociferously denied that there was any such problem, Wordham persisted until a more honest investigation established that, indeed, there was a major problem and it was fixed. Without question, Wordham saved many American lives.

With three years remaining in the decade Army Chief of Staff Harold K. Johnson said it would take to defeat North Vietnam within the strategic straitjacket imposed by the McNamara regime, and when only half of the million-man U.S. expeditionary force Johnson said would be required had been deployed, the United States deserted its South Vietnamese ally.

Initially, powerful voices in American journalism claimed that the reporters of print and broadcast had brought about that abandonment.

"The reporters and the cameras," James Reston of the *New York Times* wrote as North Vietnamese armored columns overran South Vietnam, "forced the withdrawal of American power from Vietnam."[50]

William J. Small, then director of CBS News in Washington, claimed that television news had "caused the disillusionment of Americans with this war, the cynicism of many young people towards America, and the destruction of Lyndon Johnson's tenure of office."[51]

NOTES

1. Hanson W. Baldwin, conversations with author at Carlisle Barracks, Pennsylvania, and at Baldwin's home in Connecticut, 1977–79, during preparation of a U.S. Army War College monograph, *Press Coverage of the Vietnam War: The Third View*, published in May 1979.

2. For the *Times*'s influence on all the rest of American journalism, see inter alia, Edward J. Epstein, *News from Nowhere* (New York: 1973); Random House, John Hohenberg, *Foreign Correspondence: The Great Reporters and Their Times* (New York: Columbia University, 1964); Leon V. Sigal, *Reporters and Officials: The Organization and Politics of Newsmaking* (Lexington, Mass.: D. C. Heath & Co., 1973).

3. Hanson W. Baldwin, correspondence with author, 2 August 1979.

4. Hanson W. Baldwin, "Memorandum for Mr. E.C. Daniel," 29 December 1966.

5. Clifton Daniel, "Memorandum for Mr. Baldwin," 28 December 1966.

6. Hanson Weightman Baldwin, "Reminiscences," U.S. Naval Institute Oral History Program, February–December, 1975, vols. I and II, tape no. 8, transcript p. 745.

7. Ibid., pp. 744–45.

8. U.S. Congress, Senate, Committee on Governmental Affairs, 102d Congress, 1st Session, 20 February 1991 (testimony re military-media relations).

9. Naval Institute interview, tape no. 6, transcript p. 550.

10. Naval Institute interview, tape no. 6, transcript p. 742.

11. Arthur Sylvester, "The Government Has the Right to Lie," *Saturday Evening Post*, 18 November 1967, 10–11 (an expansion of remarks made in 1962).

12. "Steve Early's Job Is to Muzzle the Loud-Mouth Brass in Pentagon," *Washington Daily News*, 18 April 1949.

13. General T. R. Milton, U.S. Air Force, a member of a group assigned by President John F. Kennedy to assess means of preventing a Communist takeover of South Vietnam, recalls that "The Green Berets were the New Frontier's answer to massive retaliation [an Eisenhower administration strategic formula and] . . . Vietnam seemed a good place to test the theory. There were no clear-cut objectives—just go over there and straighten things out." T. R. Milton, "How We Backed into Vietnam," *Air Force* 72 (May 1978):33. *Army* magazine published numerous articles, by Henry Kissinger and others, during the final years of the Eisenhower administration proposing that groups such as the Special Forces (Green Berets) be the military core of a counterinsurgency doctrine that, supposedly, would preclude intervention by large conventional military forces.

14. " 'The Tuesday luncheons were where the really important issues regarding Vietnam were discussed in great detail. We were always talking about ways and things to do with the bombing. This was where the real decisions were made.' " Dean Rusk, Johnson administration secretary of state, quoted in Leon V. Sigal, *Reporters and Officials: The Organization and Politics of Newsmaking*, (Lexington, Mass.: D. C. Heath & Co., 1973), 147.

15. Quoted from Robert J. Art, *TFX Decision: McNamara and the Military* (Boston: Little, Brown, 1968); see also U.S. Congress, Senate Committee on Government Operations, Permanent Subcommittee on Investigations, *TFX Contract Investigation Report* (Washington, D.C.: Government Printing Office, 18 December 1970).

16. Clark Mollenhoff in *The Press in Washington*, ed. Ray Eldon Hiebert (New York: Dodd, Mead & Co.), 206.

17. Richard L. Strout, "Mr. McNamara's Ordeal" (Editorial) *Christian Science Monitor*, 19 March 1963.

18. Walter Lippmann, "McNamara and the TFX," *Washington Post*, 21 March 1963.

19. "Dangerous Fight over the TFX" (Editorial) *Philadelphia Inquirer*, 22 March 1963.

20. James Reston, Commentary, Op Ed *New York Times*, 15 May 1963, p. 38.

21. "Admirals Chart Doubtful Course," (Editorial), *Denver Post*, 1 November 1965.

22. Richard Fryklund, "How One Man Shapes a War," *Washington Star*, 27 July 1965, p. 28.

23. "Before any combat ground units were sent to Vietnam I wrote a magazine article . . . estimating that it might require a million men . . . and many years to eradicate the guerrilla war and stabilize the situation. This figure was not taken out of

the air. . . . The men most directly involved—Gen. Earle G. Wheeler, Gen. Harold K. Johnson, Gen. Wallace M. Greene Jr. [all members or former members of the Joint Chiefs of Staff]—had made estimates of this magnitude, not only in talks with me, but in private speeches and discussions. I asked each one of them if these estimates had been put on paper and had been sent to the White House: their answer was 'Yes'. . . " Hanson W. Baldwin, Letter, *Army* (September 1975): 2. As early as March 25, 1964, Baldwin found it necessary to write an internal memorandum to A. O. Sulzberger, protesting delay and suppression.

24. "McNamara Pushes for Efficiency" (Editorial), *Houston Chronicle*, 31 January 1966, p. 7F.

25. "F–111 Blunder Ought to Bring Searching Quiz" (Editorial), *Louisville Courier-Journal*, 30 March 1970.

26. "McNamara and the F–111: A Chronicle of Futility," *Washington Post*, 26 April 1970, p. 27.

27. Clark R. Mollenhoff in *The Press in Washington*, ed. Ray Eldon Hiebert (New York: Dodd Mead & Co., 1967), 204, 207.

28. David Halberstam, *The Making of a Quagmire* (New York: Random House, 1975), 83.

29. Peter Arnett, "Tet Coverage: A Debate Renewed," *Columbia Journalism Review* (January–February 1978): 44–45.

30. "Recollections of Ap Bac" (Appendix B), in *Press Coverage of the Vietnam War: The Third View*: (Carlisle Barracks, Pa.: U.S. Army War College Strategic Studies Institute, 25 May 1979).

31. Marguerite Higgins, *Our Vietnam Nightmare* (New York: Harper & Row, 1965).

32. " 'I hope that your government will take a realistic look at these young generals plotting to take my place. How much maturity or political understanding do they have—of their own country, let alone the world? I am afraid there are no George Washingtons among our military. . . . Anyone who comes after me will have to resort to the same methods [regarding security and surveillance].' " President Ngo Dinh Diem to Marguerite Higgins, quoted in Higgins, *Our Vietnam Nightmare*, 169. Higgins notes (p. 229) that "Martial law was invoked more often in the two years following Diem's death than in the entire nine years of his rule!"

33. Keyes Beech, "Some Observations on Vietnam" (Appendix A), in *Press Coverage of the Vietnam War: The Third View*.

34. Roger Hilsman, "How Kennedy Viewed the Vietnam Conflict" (Letter), *New York Times*, 20 January 1992 (Hilsman served as assistant secretary of state for Far Eastern Affairs in the Kennedy administration); "Kennedy Would Have Stood by Vietnam in '65," (Letters) Wolf Lehmann, *New York Times*, 13 February 1992 (Lehmann was deputy chief of mission in the U.S. Embassy in Saigon) and W. W. Rostow, Letter, *New York Times*, 13 February 1992 (Rostow was a principal Kennedy adviser).

35. Halberstam, *Making of a Quagmire*, 315, 319, 322.

36. Neil Sheehan, correspondence with Hanson W. Baldwin, 14 September 1966.

37. General Paul D. Harkins, correspondence with author, August 1978–July 1979; General William C. Westmoreland noted with approval that "a respected Australian journalist, Denis Warner, had noted, 'there are those who say it was the first war in history lost in the columns of the *New York Times*.' " William C. Westmoreland, *A Soldier Reports* (New York: Doubleday, 1978), 420.

38. Hanson W. Baldwin, Letter, *Army* (September 1975): 2. Baldwin states that not only Johnson but also the Commandant of the Marine Corps and the Chairman of the Joint Chiefs of Staff had arrived at the same estimate, and that all three, in talks with Baldwin at the time, had formally notified the President of those estimates and had discussed them in "private speeches."

39. Johnson's warning, in 1965, got virtually no notice in the press. It appeared in print a year later in the twelfth paragraph of a thirteen paragraph story in the *Kansas City Star* ("U.S. Troops May Go Up to 750,000," 14 August 1966).

40. Naval Institute interview, tape no. 3, transcript p. 260.

41. Jo Thomas, "Bloody Ireland," *Columbia Journalism Review* 27 (May–June 1988): 32.

42. Naval Institute Oral History Interview No. 8 (743).

43. Ibid.

44. Hanson W. Baldwin, Correspondence with the author, 4 May 1978.

45. Max Frankel, correspondence with author, 4 May 1978.;

46. *Fighting for Air Time* (New York: Simon & Schuster, 1991), 135.

47. Ronald A. Roberge, interview with author, U.S. Army War College, Carlisle Barricks, Pa., 19 October 1977.

48. John McLaughlin, "Public Regulation and the News Media," *America* 107 (December 13, 1969): 587.

49. "Television reporters in Vietnam are acutely aware that what their New York offices want, above all, are action stories. . . . They are not as a rule told this in so many words. They simply know from experience what is most likely to be used . . . and for a reporter whose professional reputation (and a portion of his income) is made by what is used . . . words are unnecessary. Mike Wallace said that during the time he was in Vietnam, 'some of the correspondents kept a kind of scorecard as to which pieces were used and were not used and why, and it did seem as though an inordinate number of combat pieces were used compared with some first-rate pieces in the political area or [other] non-bloody stories.' " Dale Minor, *The Information War* (New York: Hawthorne, 1970), 155. Wallace was quoted from "The Whole World Is Watching," Public Broadcast Laboratory, 1968.

50. James Reston, "The End of the Tunnel" (Op-Ed), *New York Times*, 30 April 1975.

51. William Small, quoted in Epstein, *News from Nowhere*, 9.

8

Aftermath

Even as he fairly boasted that the reporters "forced the withdrawal of American power from Vietnam," James Reston of the *New York Times* expressed a note of apprehension. The reporters also, Reston wrote, "are now being blamed for the defeat of American policy and power in Indochina."[1]

Slaughter on a horrific scale in Cambodia belied journalistic assurances that no "bloodbath" would follow a Communist victory in Indochina. Scarcely lower on the scale of horror were unending tales of mass tragedy as tens of thousands of South Vietnamese chose the perils of the South China Sea and of robbery, rape, and murder at the hands of pirates over life under Communist rule.

American journalism became more and more uncomfortable with the exultation of such as Reston and Small over the U.S. and South Vietnamese defeat.

It found a most unlikely savior.

I first met Harry Summers when he was serving as a lieutenant colonel on the Army staff in the Pentagon and I was serving with that staff as a Reserve officer. I liked and, in the main, respected him.

An infantry combat veteran of Korea and Vietnam, Summers had returned as a staff officer during the last days of the Vietnam debacle and had dealt directly with North Vietnamese army counterparts in the sporadic "peace" negotiations. I found him to be intelligent and articulate, but tinged with the old Pentagon staff officer's greatest weakness—a tendency to tell the boss what he wants to hear. Our paths were to cross on other grounds.

In November 1978, General Walter T. Kerwin, Jr., then vice chief of staff of the Army, had ordered that a study be done to find out what went wrong in Vietnam.[2] The strictly historical aspects of the study were contracted to

BDM, Inc., a military consulting firm, of McLean, Virginia. Substudies dealing with "public support for strategies" and "decisions regarding mobilization" were to be performed within the U.S. Army War College Strategic Studies Institute at Carlisle Barracks, Pennsylvania. As a civilian member of the Strategic Studies Institute at that time, I was assigned the task relating to public support.

General Kerwin's wish was that the study be given the widest possible public exposure. To that end, it was determined from the beginning that the final study report would be written by one author, thereby avoiding the deadening prose of the committee-produced product.

An important study dealing with military-media relations already had been done at the War College, in 1969, by three lieutenant colonels and a colonel who had fought as battalion commanders in the 1968 Tet Offensive in Vietnam.[3] That study was based on a statistical analysis of Tet coverage by the major national media, print and broadcast. It concluded "that the Tet Offensive was an Allied victory . . . portrayed inaccurately to the American people and thereby [it] resulted in a psychological defeat. . . . Allied victory in Vietnam is adjudged from the disproportionate and awesome military losses suffered by the enemy; the favorable performance of the South Vietnamese Armed Forces; the failure of the people to support the Viet Cong; and the endurance in adversity . . . evidenced by the Government of South Vietnam."[4]

All subsequent studies, civilian as well as military, from whatever point of view have supported those findings.

Informed of the study started by General Kerwin, Hanson W. Baldwin, by then retired from the New York Times, authorized unlimited access to and publication of the large numbers of internal Times documents and related papers he had deposited at Yale University. He also made himself available for extensive interviews and correspondence.

Numerous other Vietnam-era journalists were interviewed during media-military seminars in the regular War College curriculum. These included Peter Arnett, then of the AP; Gloria Emerson, formerly of the New York Times; several television network correspondents; and editors, correspondents, or former correspondents of Newsweek and Time.

There were discussions with editors of the Washington Post and with the chief executives and editors of the AP. The extensive papers willed to Syracuse University by Marguerite Higgins were also studied.

From these and other efforts during the first several months of study it was apparent that the extreme "pro" and "anti" aspects of the military-press relationship were clearly enough established in the public domain and required no further elucidation. What had not been clarified was the existence of a middle ground, a "third view" that represented the viewpoint of journalists who were critical of both the government and the press. This third view was held by virtually all reporters who had extensive prior experience in covering military affairs, notably Baldwin; Higgins; Keyes Beech of the *Chicago Daily News*, and later of the *Los Angeles Times*; Jim G. Lucas of the Scripps-Howard newspapers; and S. L. A. Marshall of the *Detroit News*.

A draft study report was prepared on the basis of this initial effort and submitted to the War College for review and discussion by a panel of major military and press figures from the Vietnam era. These included Major General Winant Sidle, former military press chief in Saigon and later in Washington; Lee Lescaze, then of the *Washington Post*; and Neil Sheehan, by then departed from the *New York Times* to write what would eventually be published as *A Bright Shining Lie*.

None of the reviewers challenged the draft in any substantial respect. It was published in May 1979 as a War College monograph under the title *Press Coverage of the Vietnam War: The Third View.*[5] Much of the substance of that monograph appears in various chapters of this book, mainly in Chapter 7.

Thus, there were now on public record two War College studies that raised grave questions about the competence of press coverage during the Vietnam War.

During the final phase of the War College press substudy, Harry Summers, by then promoted to colonel, was assigned to the Strategic Studies Institute to write the final Vietnam study report. By this time the BDM effort had been completed and published in six volumes.

Inexplicably—at least it seemed so initially—Summers's report, published as *On Strategy*,[6] not only ignored the criticism of the press contained in the two War College studies, but also exonerated the press from any blame whatsoever for the Vietnam disaster. Both the 1969 Tet Offensive study and the 1979 monograph had been widely distributed. When none of the criticism contained in those documents was so much as mentioned in what the press knew to be the final Vietnam study report, the press was euphoric.

Immediately upon the appearance of the commercial version of *On Strategy*, CBS television went on the air with an adulatory report (July 11, 1983). Lest the viewer not be bright enough to get the full import of the book, it was pointed out in vivid terms that it was not "a stab in the back . . . by an unpatriotic press" that lost the war, but rather the failure of the U.S. military to tell the government and the public what was wrong with the war. No mention was made of the fate of General Decker and Admiral Anderson when they did attempt to warn the public or of the warning by General Johnson that nothing less than a million men and ten years would be required.

Bright and early the next day, anchor Dan Rather followed up on CBS radio. He modestly admitted that, while *On Strategy* gave him no cause for embarrassment, he himself had made some mistakes as a correspondent in Vietnam, but ascribed these to the Army's failure to make it plain to him beforehand that war was "mud and blood."

It took John McWethy of ABC somewhat longer to get his feelings of exaltation and exculpation on record, but he did so in a letter criticizing one of a drumfire of articles damning press coverage in Vietnam that had been appearing in the professional military press for at least a decade. Thus, in the October 1984 issue of *U.S. Naval Institute Proceedings*, McWethy concluded his rebuttals by quoting Summers's grant of general absolution in *On Strategy*:

There is a tendency in the military to blame our problems with public support on the media. . . . The majority of the on-the-scene reporting from Vietnam was factual— that is, reporters honestly reported what they had seen firsthand. Much of what they saw was horrible, for that is the true nature of war. It was this horror, not the reporting that so influenced the American people.

In fact, there was no evidence then, and is none now, to support this theory of a television-induced collapse of will on the part of the American public, millions of whom had seen at first hand or had heard from veterans of those conflicts horrors on a much greater scale in World War II and Korea. On the contrary, all of the public opinion evidence subsequently gathered by Burns W. Roper[7] and other analysts indicates that television had no impact whatsoever on the public at large, although it did have enormous impact on Washington decision makers, in particular President Johnson, Secretary McNamara, and those around the president who *assumed* that the public was as dismayed as they were by the sensationalistic television reporting. In fact, says Roper, the public gave up on the war only after Johnson, McNamara, and McNamara's "whiz kids" in effect surrendered in March 1968 on the basis of the alarmist, and erroneous, Tet Offensive reporting.

Ironically, Summers had stumbled into affirming what his former military colleagues had long since concluded—that the war was lost on television— and they were preparing to do something about that.

The truth of the matter is that television reporting in Vietnam was utterly irrelevant to the outcome of the war, one way or the other. That final outcome had been decided in the main in 1963 when the overthrow and murder of President Diem destroyed the only legitimate political base there had ever been for the war. From that point on, as General Johnson tried to explain to his president and his countrymen, all that a million-man, ten-year effort could hope to achieve were the exhaustion of North Vietnam and the preservation of a corrupt, U.S.-installed regime in South Vietnam under the protection of a huge, long-term U.S. garrison. Americans would have fought on even for that, Burns Roper concluded, if President Johnson had stayed the course.

Just as misreporting of the complex Diem issues had led President Kennedy to a disastrous decision in 1963, so misreporting of the 1968 Tet Offensive led to the collapse of will on the part of President Johnson and of the McNamara coterie in the Pentagon. Ironically, Roper and others have long since established through analysis of the postelection polling that the immediate cause of Johnson's moral collapse—the heavy vote for a Democratic opponent, Eugene McCarthy, in the 1968 New Hampshire primary— was similarly misreported and misinterpreted by the press.[8] That is, the voters who supported McCarthy in the primary mainly voted in the general election for Alabama Governor George Wallace on a "win the war" platform. On that same platform was none other than the world's leading advocate of bombing the North Vietnamese "back into the Stone Age," retired Air Force General Curtis E. LeMay. In short, the New Hampshire primary voters were trying to throw out a president who would not prosecute the war to a conclusion and replace him with one who talked in terms of "victory."

Dan Rather's charge that the military failed to alert the public, presumably by resignations, had become a subject of intense discussion and debate within the military itself. In the mind of General William C. Westmoreland, the principal U.S commander in Vietnam, the fulsome support from the press for the firing of Decker and Anderson seemed to indicate that "the American people" did not want senior officers defying civilian authority in any form.[9] Even so, Westmoreland came to believe that resignation would have been better than permitting himself to be used as a military front for Kennedy, Johnson, and McNamara policies that had foredoomed the effort.

The *New York Times* greeted Colonel Harry Summers's *On Strategy* by offering him a job, in effect as replacement for Hanson Baldwin. Summers accepted instead an offer from *U.S. News and World Report* and from there went on to become a syndicated columnist for the Los Angeles Times News Service, but retaining all the while an official connection as a "Distinguished Fellow of the U.S. Army War College." Although this was a blatant conflict of interest, the press was so relieved and delighted over Summers's exculpation of its Vietnam performance that the issue has never been raised.

On February 20, 1991, Summers appeared in a televised hearing before a subcommittee of the House Committee on Government Affairs and denounced both Harrison Salisbury and Peter Arnett for treason, a charge he would repeat in his syndicated column. As the basis for his charge against Salisbury Summers cited the 1966 trip to Hanoi, the full details of which he had literally on his desk in the form of the Army War College press substudy when he wrote the press a clean bill of health in *On Strategy*. He had similarly ignored, in *On Strategy*, the extensive criticism of Arnett's Diem episode and Tet Offensive reporting contained in the War College press substudy and the earlier Tet Offensive study by the four former battalion commanders. Although no one had accused Arnett of treason in those studies, his reporting from Baghdad during the Persian Gulf War, which formed the basis of Summers's charge, was indistinguishable on moral and professional bases from his Vietnam reporting.

On Strategy effectively insulated the press less against criticism than against self-criticism. It now saw itself as vindicated. Had not the Army itself established that the basic structure of American journalism was sound and that it was accepted as the true servant—indeed, the alter ego—of the public?

In 1982, even as *On Strategy* was beginning to come to public attention, the seeds of disillusion were sown.

A moth-eaten old British lion, propped up on every side by President Ronald Reagan and other worshipful Americans, embarked on an imperial foray to recapture the Falklands/Malvinas Islands, seized during a foolish Argentine military adventure.

From beginning to end, however, the British government kept the press absolutely under control. Embarked on warships or tightly grouped under the Official Secrets Act in London, the press was permitted to transmit only what would serve the government's interests. From afar, U.S. Navy officers looked on, admired, and learned.

In the May–June 1983 issue of *Naval War College Review*, Lieutenant Commander Arthur A. Humphries, a member of a Naval War College group set up to study the lessons of the Falklands/Malvinas campaign, warned that

1. "To maintain popular support for a war, your side must not be seen as ruthless barbarians;

2. "If you don't want to erode the public's confidence in the government's war aims, then you cannot allow that public's sons to be wounded and maimed right in front of them via their TV sets at home;

3. "You must, therefore, control correspondents' access to the fighting."[10]

Four months later, a U.S. joint task force was ordered to seize the island of Grenada. The joint task force commander, Vice Admiral Joseph Metcalf III, put into effect a public affairs policy that was virtually word for word out of Commander Humphries' article. The press was simply and totally excluded until the military was satisfied that it could do no harm.

A howl of rage went up from the aggrieved editors and broadcasters. Then they got the shock of their lives. By every means open to them—letters to the editor, calls to radio talk shows, communications with Congress, responses to public opinion polls—the public made it known that it backed Admiral Metcalf to the hilt.[11]

Was this the public for which the press had claimed to speak throughout the latter stages of the Vietnam War? No. It was the public whose devotion to the armed services in time of danger, whose steadfastness in the face of loss and hardship, and whose contempt for half measures *both* the press and the military had totally misread in their shared belief, utterly without foundation, scientific or otherwise, that it was the public, not their leaders, who had caved in to enemy pressure as portrayed through television in Vietnam.

So shocked was the press by the degree of hostility it was encountering from the public that it stumbled into what it would later recognize to have been a trap.[12]

The Department of Defense had graciously offered to remedy its "mistake" in the handling of Grenada press relations by appointing a thirteen-member commission to devise procedures to assure early access by the press in any future military action "to the maximum degree possible consistent with the security of the mission and the safety of troops."[13] The chairman of the group was the former highest-ranking uniformed Department of Defense press spokesman during the latter phase of the Vietnam War, now become a public relations executive for a major defense contractor. All members of the commission, civilian as well as military, were handpicked by the chairman of the Joint Chiefs of Staff.

Anyone innocent enough to believe that such an aggregation was going to make it easier for the press to cover a war should not be permitted out of the house unescorted. It was a measure of the press's disarray that it swallowed the commission's remedy, hook, line, and sinker.

That remedy was to create a "pool" of journalists, allotted by various formulas among newspapers, the news magazines, television, and the wire services, who were to be alerted by the Department of Defense whenever U.S. forces were to be sent into combat and permitted to accompany the assault forces. The press would get to name the members of the pool. The responsibility for everything else from the first alert to the moment the pool stepped ashore on hostile or recently hostile territory, and to an undefined degree thereafter, would remain firmly in the hands of the government.

How that would work out was displayed for all the world to see when units of the 82d Airborne Division were sent to Honduras, in February 1987, to make a mass parachute jump intended to warn the then Communist government of Nicaragua of what the Reagan administration might have in store for it. The Washington press pool was duly alerted and accompanied a lead element of the paratroopers. With representatives of the world press assembled along the edge of the drop zone, the paratroopers jumped, but not the press pool. They continued to ride along in the military transports until a less arduous landing was made at the nearby Palmerolo Air Base. They got back out to the drop zone some time later under close military escort, behind convoys of water trailers and other higher-priority items.

Neither the members of the pool nor the assembled world press prepositioned at the drop zone got the message.

A feeling that all was not well with the pool idea began to emerge in 1987–88 when the pool system was used to rotate members of the press to U.S. warships escorting Kuwait tankers in the Persian Gulf. "The current system of pool coverage is not efficient," a *New York Times* reporter would lament. "Most of a typical three-week rotation . . . is spent ashore, with little to do. Our group became so frustrated with the leisurely life at the Diplomat Hotel in Bahrain that we had tee-shirts printed with the slogan: 'When there's news in the Gulf, we're in the pool.' "[14]

What the Defense Department had in mind became much clearer when the Washington pool was alerted once again to accompany U.S. troops invading Panama in January 1989. Exactly as had happened in February 1987, in Honduras, the pool got to accompany the assault elements alright, but once the paratroopers had left the plane, the pool stayed with the aircraft, landed at a secure airport, and remained in the airport lounge until the military was sufficiently satisfied with developments that it was willing to let the reporters go out more or less on their own.

By now the publicly expressed complaints of the press over such treatment were much more muted than had been the case at the time of the Grenada invasion. Nothing had changed to lead anyone in either the press or the Defense Department to doubt that public support remained solidly with the military. But, for the first time since Harry Summers's *On Strategy* had effectively stifled internal press dissent, an important critical voice was raised within the press itself.

From a hotel room in Rome, columnist and long-term Latin America specialist Georgie Anne Geyer viewed with astonishment a report by CNN and a column by Tom Wicker of the *New York Times* blaming the United States for destruction of a Panama slum neighborhood when her own first-hand reporting, confirmed by a study by the Catholic church, identified Cuban-trained forces loyal to Panamanian dictator Manuel Noriega as the culprits. "A dangerous vacuity characterized far too much of this coverage," and other television postinvasion reports, Geyer wrote. "Responsibility . . . is [not] a word pertinent to much of our coverage."[15]

What is most striking about the behavior of the press from the time it ran into a post-Grenada wall of public hostility throughout the early pool deployments and the Panama invasion is that it looked solely and entirely to the government for a solution to its problems of wartime coverage. It was the government that must devise a system by which the press could get to the scene of action. It was the government that must make all of the physical arrangements. It was the government that must provide the information that would enable the pool members to understand what the deployment was all about and the nature of the troops they would be accompanying and to arrange upon arrival for explanations of what was going on, weapons being used, and so on. All of this was to be done at public expense, with the press to pocket the monetary returns.

Interestingly enough, the only suggestion that there might be a better way of doing things came not from the press, but from the U.S. Southern Command Public Affairs Office in Panama subsequent to the 1989 invasion. Wouldn't it be better, the Southern Command asked, to use reporters who were already on the scene, who were regularly assigned to Panama and the resident U.S. military units? After all, most or all spoke Spanish, had some acquaintance with the U.S. military, and were fairly knowledgeable about the country. Also, they were there—and likely to be somewhat fresher and better oriented than would be Washington reporters possibly roused out in the middle of the night and subjected to a long flight under conditions considerably removed from the first-class travel to which they were accustomed.

That idea, predictably, got nowhere. The Department of Defense did not want reporters covering a war who knew more about what was going on than did the Secretary of Defense and the president, and a press that believes the cream of journalistic talent is gathered in Washington and New York wanted no local talent disturbing that notion. So, for oddly different reasons, the government and the press had more or less wandered into a working relationship that served the political interests of the governing administration and the institutional interests, or at least the egos and illusions, of both parties at the expense of the public they both claimed to serve.

The pool arrangement would get its first test in full-scale war in the Persian Gulf in 1990–91. The result would be a military establishment more firmly in control of how it is covered by the press than at any time in its history and a press reduced virtually to the status of a court jester. Yet, there was no need to have anyone on the ground in August 1990, when the United States decided to challenge the Iraqi occupation of Kuwait, to transmit to the American public an accurate understanding of the dangerous situation it was confronting.

If competent researchers had been backing up even the handful of full-time correspondents covering the Pentagon, someone almost certainly would have noted a Congressional Budget Office Persian Gulf deployment study that had resurfaced only a few weeks before, in May.[16] That study made it plain how long it would take for the U.S. military to deploy a force adequate to counter the Iraqi armored divisions that were available in Kuwait, poised to move into Saudi Arabia.

In fact, the only such long-term research center that had ever been built up in an American journalistic enterprise had been destroyed in the internal *New York Times* disputes that preceded the retirement of Hanson W. Baldwin as military editor, some twenty years earlier, never to be replaced at the *Times* or anywhere else.

So between the time when the first lightly armed U.S. paratroopers and Marines arrived in Saudi Arabia in August and that when a reasonably strong allied covering force had been created in October no one told the U.S. or world public that only the implied threat of nuclear weapons stood between those first U.S. forces to arrive and an Iraqi prison camp, with the enormous leverage that would have given the Iraqis. The press stumbled all around that crucially important story without recognizing its full dimensions.

"Pentagon Faces Daunting Challenge in Rushing Sizable Force to Mideast," the *New York Times* told its readers on August 14, 1990, in a story by Eric Schmitt. "[T]he deployment of forces to Saudi Arabia is rushing forward, spurred by concerns that a sizable ground force be landed there before Iraq can begin a wide attack." Ironically, a "box" next to the story listed exactly the U.S. units that had been considered in the 1983 Congressional Budget Office study that had documented the enormity of the logistical effort required before such a force could be gotten into place and sustained in major combat operations. As to when Iraq could "begin a wide attack," it was in position to do so from the moment its armored divisions occupied Kuwait.

Whatever else Schmitt and his editors missed in that article, they did not pass up the opportunity to reinforce a longstanding *Times* editorial policy opposing the Strategic Defense Initiative ("Star Wars"): "The movement of forces to Saudi Arabia raises questions about the Government's commitment to less flashy military programs, which unlike the 'Star Wars' program . . . garner little attention. . . . " Had every cent spent to that date on the Strategic Defense Initiative been spent instead on airlift and sealift, time and distance still would have precluded timely interposition of an adequate U.S. covering force between the Iraqis and the Saudi ports and airfields. Assuming Iraq ever had any intention of moving into Saudi Arabia, the threat of a nuclear response is the only conceivable element of military power that could have stopped them.

As late as May 5, 1991, the *Times* would acknowledge in an editorial that "The President personally committed himself to protecting Saudi Arabia [on August 3, 1990] long before sufficient U.S. forces could be positioned in the gulf." The full implications still had not dawned.

Some months after the war, magazine writer Richard Mackenzie said to Lieutenant General Charles A. Horner, Air Force commander in the Persian Gulf War, "I understand that, among the three or four [U.S.] generals [in Saudi Arabia on August 5] the only weapon was a pocketknife."

"John Yeosock [the senior Army general present] had it," General Horner answered. "One night I said to him, 'Jack, what have you got to defend us?' He pulled out his pocketknife. That was it."[17]

David Evans, a retired Marine lieutenant colonel reporting for the *Chicago Tribune*, reported even while the war was in progress that "Some of the first Army units into Saudi Arabia, including the 82d Airborne, found themselves asking the Marines for rations, validating the observation of one [Marine] colonel that the combat-ready—but lightly supported—Army paratroopers are 'a bunch of guys who show up with their bag lunches looking for dinner.' "[18] Had Evans been less the prisoner of his own service background, he would have recorded that the Marines were no better equipped to defend Saudi Arabia against a large-scale armored assault than were the Army paratroopers. Evans, also, never asked what it was that could have stopped such an assault, whether that threat had deterred the Iraqis, and what that meant for the American constitutional process with respect to initiation of nuclear war.

Four months into the Saudi buildup, the situation was still so serious that Lieutenant General Calvin A. H. Waller, the second-highest-ranking U.S. officer in the Persian Gulf, took the unprecedented action of issuing a public warning that it would take additional weeks to build up an adequate allied force for offensive action. This was in response to pressure from political authority in Washington for quicker action.

In the aftermath of Vietnam, the press had castigated the military leadership of that era for not having taken such risky, career-endangering action to warn the public against incompetent political leadership. Yet the plaudits for Waller were few and far between. *Newsweek*, long after the war, would sneer that Waller had "blurted out" his warning.

Saudi Arabia presented the most difficult imaginable challenge to reporting the allied buildup. While President Diem of South Vietnam had given American journalists the run of the country, and had paid for it with his life, the Saudi royal family had never been tempted to permit such an opening. As a result, there were no established U.S. press representatives on the ground when U.S. troops began to arrive.

Now the full implications of the pool arrangement began to dawn on the American press. In agreeing to the Washington-based press pool, the publishers and broadcasters had played into the hands of the Department of Defense news managers by assuring that in any major deployment the Washington journalists would not accompany the key military headquarters involved. That is, by the time the Washington journalists were notified and assembled, the controlling headquarters, never likely to be located in Washington, would long since have departed. Thus, while the Washington press pool got off on August 13, only one day after President George Bush had ordered U.S. forces to Saudi Arabia, the advance elements of the controlling headquarters—U.S. Central Command at McDill Air Force Base in Florida—were long gone.

The press had been neither quick enough nor perceptive enough to understand the implications of what the U.S. Southern Command Public Affairs Office had suggested eight months before, during the Panama invasion. That is, had the press, even at that late date, assigned to each major U.S. joint military command at least one full-time reporter, he or she would have been able to gain an understanding of the command's mission, of the forces assigned, and of the geographic area or function for which it was responsible, and, most important, he or she would have been able to develop a working relationship. It then would have been difficult, most likely impossible, for the Defense Department managers in Washington to argue that the reporter on the command beat could not be given the one seat necessary to permit accompanying coverage of the command from the moment it left the United States.

As it was, the Washington pool arrangement made beggars and supplicants of the press. The collective ignorance of the assigned reporters regarding every aspect of the command, forces to be deployed, characteristics of the theater of operations, and so on made them a burden on the military, and on the public, at a time when the time of responsible officials and transportation resources could not be spared from more urgent matters.

The pool operated throughout under close military escort, at a carefully controlled distance from the most important news sources. All news copy and pictures could be transmitted only through the military escort officers, via communications under military or Saudi control.

Nominally, the pool was disbanded on August 26. By that time, however, sufficient Department of Defense military press managers had been deployed to maintain essentially the same degree of control over the activities of the hundreds of media representatives who were converging on Saudi Arabia from throughout the world. These were effectively concentrated in hotels, their access to military units carefully controlled by a set of Department of Defense guidelines. Backing up the guidelines was a Saudi threat to withdraw the visa of any reporter who transgressed.[19]

Although the Department of Defense pool, as such, had been disbanded in August, virtually all subsequent coverage of the war was managed by various types of pool arrangements controlled from a military Joint Information Bureau. These effectively turned the press against itself, as reporters jockeyed for positions in the pools and reported on colleagues who tried to get around the pool arrangement by attempting to visit military units and other potential news sources on their own. The performance made a mockery of journalists' claims to be members of a "profession."

Although not intended, or at least not foreseen as such by the Department of Defense, the military's most powerful means of control of the press proved to be the daily televised press briefings in Washington and in Saudi Arabia. The contrast between well-groomed, neatly uniformed, confident, polite, and well-informed senior military officers and an often unkempt, rude, and absurdly ill-prepared press was devastating.

Once again in her new and unexpected role as press critic, columnist Georgie Anne Geyer summed up the press performance in the briefings: "Adversarial antagonism toward just about everybody, self-satisfied arrogance in the face of authority, and finally . . . incredible ignorance about other cultures and war. . . . That has been what the public has seen. . . ."[20]

Richard Harwood, a longtime senior editor of the *Washington Post*, supported that view: "Too many unprepared and dull-witted reporters demonstrated their incompetence day after day to television audiences throughout the world."[21]

Not since the silencing of Marguerite Higgins and Hanson W. Baldwin had such criticism from distinguished sources arisen within the press itself.

The senior military briefer in Washington, personable Lieutenant General Thomas W. Kelly, identified very quickly those reporters who knew least about the military and the theater of operations and thereafter was careful to give them preference as to the questions he accepted.

A different version of that same theme was played out in Saudi Arabia. In the fifteen years between the end of U.S. involvement in Vietnam and the beginning of the Gulf War only one journalist who did not carry the professional and emotional baggage of the retired military officer had gained at least a foothold as a syndicated columnist specializing in military affairs. That was Fred Reed, whose weekly column was distributed by Universal Press Syndicate. A Vietnam veteran who had educated himself in the details of military technology, Reed was well known in the military as a sometimes acerbic, but knowledgeable, critic who followed no service or political party line. When he attempted to cover the Persian Gulf War, the Joint Information Bureau so effectively isolated him from any contact whatsoever with U.S. military units that he gave up his column in disgust.[22]

This dual policy of catering to the ignorant and excluding the knowledgeable worked so well that the principal military briefer in Saudi Arabia, Marine Brigadier General R. I. Neal, could tell a conference of newspaper editors in Boston after the war that their reporters "didn't lay a glove on him. . . . They never asked the hard questions he spent four to five hours a day preparing to answer."[23]

To compound the daily humiliations the press was bringing down on itself in the televised briefings, both the networks and the leading newspapers advertised their failure to develop journalists capable of informed, independent analysis by hiring a collection of retired generals and civilian think-tankers as "experts." For the first time since W. H. Russell of the *London Times* began the modern tradition of independent military journalism during the Crimean War, the press turned over to the generals who had written the plans for a war an international forum in which they could proclaim the brilliance of those plans. We were back, once again, to Caesar and his unchallenged self-assessment of his performance in the Gallic wars. The process was carried to the point of high humor when the *Los Angeles Times* engaged a novelist, Tom Clancy, to explain the war to its readers.

None of the network anchors who solemnly and reverently introduced their newly acquired think-tank "experts" bothered to inform the audience as to who funded those think tanks, there being no such thing as a think tank without a political or institutional axe to grind. Nor did those same anchors, usually in full cry over any real or perceived conflict of interest on the part of politicians, bother to inform the audience that one of the most prominent of their civilian "experts" was on the payroll of a U.S. senator deeply committed to the administration that was conducting the war.

The surrender of journalistic virtue that had begun with meek acceptance of the Washington press pool in 1985 was now virtually complete. The military now controlled, almost in toto, not only news of combat military operations at the source, but, through its retired officer surrogates, network and often newspaper analysis as well.

Rear Admiral Brent Baker, the Navy's chief of information, could report with satisfaction that "A *Times-Mirror* public opinion poll conducted 25 March 1991 indicated that 84 percent of the American public gave the press an excellent or good grade for Desert Storm coverage and 83 percent said military restrictions on news reports during the conflict were a good thing. A Gallup . . . poll in early 1991 showed 85 percent of the public had a high level of confidence in the military as an institution after Desert Shield/Storm. . . . Where did the public get its perception of the military's professionalism? They got it from news media reports."[24]

Not all the public, however, felt so comfortable.

"The government's censorship of press coverage," Bud A. McClure of Chambersburg, Pennslvyania, wrote in a letter to the *Harrisburg Patriot-News*, "combined with its carefully orchestrated public relations campaign to sanitize and make palatable this war [the government] is aided and abetted by the media. At Pentagon-sponsored press conferences the media sit with childlike stares entranced by spoon-fed images. . . ."[25]

Emogene Trexel, a Harrisburg attorney, felt that "In this war . . . I was robbed of my personal capacity to discern truth. . . . I, along with every other American, had been duped into believing what I was seeing and hearing through the media. The war news wasn't news. I really was a victim of my government's own propaganda."[26]

The percentages of public support for the military versus the press were not a product of the Gulf War. As early as the spring of 1985, Dr. Kirstin McGrath, president of Minnesota Opinion Research, Inc., had warned the American Society of Newspaper Editors of deep rifts between journalists and the public at large concerning fundamental beliefs ranging from religion to support of the military.[27] Concerning the latter, Dr. McGrath's pollsters had found that 80 percent of the public supported imposition of restrictions on coverage of U.S. forces during wartime.

That level of public support for military control of the press during wartime made itself apparent to pollsters in the wake of the 1983 invasion of Grenada, and it remained constant through the Persian Gulf War, enormously re-inforced by what the public saw of press behavior and lack of technical competence in the televised Gulf War briefings. The origin of the pro-military, anti-press sentiment, however, were not in Grenada, but in Vietnam.

What the overwhelming evidence of the polls and all other sources of public expression now tell us is that, had the Vietnam-era military chiefs resigned in public protest over the fatally flawed McNamara strategy, the public would have responded overwhelmingly in favor of an all-out land, sea, and air assault on North Vietnam, come what may with respect to the reaction of China and the Soviet Union. In the U.S. military's continuing misapprehension of the moral character of the American people lies a grave danger: A military elite that believes public support turns on images, or lack of images, on the television screen is only one step away from self-appointing themselves as the political as well as the military "protectors" of such weak and vulnerable sheep.

Isolated in the polls and embarrassed by their own televised incompetence, the press could make only some weak representations following the Gulf War in an effort to obtain some sort of alleviation of the pool straitjacket into which it had blundered, and which many of its executives were now acknowledging to have been a "trap." " 'This is an effort by responsible press members to see that war coverage is what the public deserves,' Louis D. Boccardi, President and Chief Executive of The Associated Press, said lamely in presenting the new proposals. As just about the last of his confreres to hold that view, Boccardi described the pool system as having been 'designed to facilitate coverage.' In fact, he had to admit, 'The pool coverage as it happened in the Gulf obstructed coverage.' "[28]

Having no one better trained for such coverage, Boccardi had sent the AP's theater critic, Jay F. Sharbutt, to cover the war. Ten months after the war Boccardi still was unable to understand that when the press sends a drama critic to cover a war, the closely controlled pool system is the only means of assuring the safety of both the reporter and the military. Indeed, it was only the quick thinking of U.S. Army Captain Frans C. Barends on the night of February 27, 1991, that saved *Minneapolis Star-Tribune* reporter Paul McEnroe from being blasted to kingdom come when McEnroe, escaping from pool supervision, drove his Land Rover between Barends' tank company and the Iraqis.[29]

Only one recourse remained to the press—to demonstrate that the restrictions imposed by the military during the war had, indeed, enabled the military to cover up gross errors and misconduct. Thus, when Patrick J. Sloyan of *Newsday* published a series supposedly exposing the heretofore unreported burying alive by the U.S. Army of "thousands" of Iraqis, he was promptly nominated for, and granted, a Pulitzer Prize.

Ordered to break through Iraqi entrenchments en route to freeing Kuwait of Iraqi occupation, U.S. front-line commanders were faced with an unpleasant choice: lead with tank-equipped bulldozers that would crush or bury alive anyone who remained in their path, or send U.S. infantrymen into those trenches and dugouts to fight it out, one on one, with hand grenades and sharpened entrenching tools.

From the time in the nineteenth century when the high-explosive shell began to dominate the battlefield, the risk of being buried alive has grown apace. That is, safety of a sort lay only in digging deeper and deeper dugouts in which to obtain some sort of fitful sleep and sweat out artillery barrages. What could and often did happen was described in a poem by Sergeant Joyce Kilmer during World War I. He recorded how members of his unit had to give up digging into the ruins of one such collapsed dugout, knowing that there were still men alive down there, but that they were unreachable with the equipment at hand.

With over a century of military history to tell them that about as many Americans as Iraqis were likely to be killed in hand-to-hand fighting in the trenches and bunkers, the U.S. assault commanders in the Gulf War opted for the bulldozers. Given the frontages along which standard U.S. doctrine dictated the penetrations would be made and the likely density of enemy defenders dictated by prudent dispersal in the face of heavy artillery concentrations, it is most unlikely that "thousands" of Iraqis were buried alive by the bulldozers. If there were thousands of Iraqi bodies in those positions, it is much more likely, again on the basis of a century of such grim experience, that they had been killed by the incessant bombing campaign of the previous week or the preassault artillery barrage, rather than by the bulldozers.

Moreover, this is not the first time that a Pulitzer Prize has been awarded more for the benefit of institutional interests than as a reward for quality journalism. David Halberstam was awarded a Pulitzer Prize less to reward the quality of his reporting from Vietnam than to silence those who were raising uncomfortable questions about the role of the *New York Times* in the overthrow and murder of President Diem. According to Hanson Baldwin, an attempt was made to silence critics of Harrison Salisbury's 1966 trip to Hanoi by awarding Salisbury a Pulitzer, but it failed by one vote.[30]

No sooner was the award to Patrick Sloyan announced than it was challenged by James S. Doyle, editorial director of the Army Times Publishing Company. The first reports, Doyle charged, "about the Iraqis buried alive in their trenches" were not by Sloyan, but "by Steve Vogel and Jim Tice of *Army Times* . . . in March, 1991. A second fuller account . . . appeared in August. Sloyan's expanded version of the incident appeared about a month later, shortly after a *Newsday* librarian requested *Army Times* copies and a *Newsday* courier got them."[31]

That Sloyan was a regular reader of *Army Times* was established from his acknowledged "pickup" of another, unrelated *Army Times* report. He had credited *Army Times* in paragraph three of the story, but, according to Sloyan, "the [*Newsday*] desk moved [it] down lower," into paragraph nine.[32]

Whatever the degree to which Sloyan's Pulitzer belonged to the *Army Times* writers, the dispute brought to the surface a longstanding fact of Washington life: Having neglected intensive coverage of national defense in Washington and elsewhere, the national press has come to rely more and more on the specialized coverage of such as Army, Navy, and Air Force *Times* and *Aviation Week and Space Technology*, usually crediting the source, if at all, in about paragraph nine or later.

It was not only *Newsday* that was embarrassed by Doyle's questioning of its Pulitzer. The *New York Times* ran its report of the episode not in the national news section, but at the bottom of page two of the Metro section, exactly as it had "buried" reports of self-immolations from Saigon when those no longer served the purpose of undermining the Diem regime. The headline, set in the smallest available headline type, identified the source of the complaint only as a "weekly," presumably from somewhere in southern Illinois.

Why? Because the *Times*, according to sources at Columbia University who do not wish to be further identified, controls the Pulitzer process. It intervenes directly only when major institutional interests are at stake, as in the Halberstam and Salisbury cases, and is content to sprinkle around awards to other major dailies—even to its last direct competitor in New York—as an aristocratic beneficence. Thus, the *Army Times* criticism of the award was as much an embarrassment to the *New York Times*, the power behind the Pulitzer scene, as it was to *Newsday*.[33]

From Grenada to the Sloyan Pulitzer, nothing has gone right for the press in its relationship to the U.S. military, but the name of that disaster is not Grenada, or Panama, or the Gulf War. It is Vietnam, and it is the result of the press's refusal to frankly assess its own role both in creating that catastrophe and in using Harry Summers's *On Strategy* to avoid making the necessary corrections.

NOTES

1. James Reston, "The End of the Tunnel," (Op Ed), *New York Times*, 30 April 1975.

2. U.S. Department of the Army, Office of the Deputy Chief of Staff for Operations and Plans, "Study Directive: Strategic Lessons Learned in Vietnam," 18 November 1978.

3. Chandler Goodnow, Louis G. Michael, Edward A. Partain, and Sidney R. Steele, "News Coverage of the Tet Offensive" (Research paper, U.S. Army War College, Carlisle Barracks, Pa., 25 March 1969).

4. Ibid.

5. William V. Kennedy, "Press Coverage of the War in Vietnam: The Third View," U.S. Army War College Strategic Studies Institute, Carlisle Barracks, Pennsylvania, 25 May 1979.

6. This was published initially as a War College document and later, in 1983, under commercial imprint by Presidio, San Francisco.

7. Burns W. Roper, "What Public Opinion Polls Said," *Big Story*, vol. 1 (Boulder, Colo.: Westview, 1977), 674–704.

8. Ibid., 671.

9. William C. Westmoreland, conversation with author, Carlisle Barracks, Pa., 1978.

10. Arthur A. Humphries, "Two Routes to the Wrong Destination: Public Affairs in the South Atlantic War," *Naval War College Review* (May–June 1983): 56–71 (emphasis added).

11. Richard M. Clurman, "The Media Learn a Lesson" (Op-Ed), *New York Times*, 2 December 1983.

12. Jonathan Friendly, "Joint Chiefs Plan New Press Policy," *New York Times*, 2 February 1984, p. A7.

13. Quoted by Jonathan Friendly, "War Zone Access by Press Affirmed," *New York Times*, 7 February 1984, p. A12.

14. Jack Cushman, "This . . . Is the Gulf," *U.S. Naval Institute Proceedings/Naval Review* 114 (1988): 50; see also Jack Cushman, "Gathering News in the Persian Gulf: Suntans and Simmering Frustration," *New York Times*, 4 January 1988, p. A14.

15. Georgie Anne Geyer, "News Coverage of Panama Erroneous," *Harrisburg* (Pa.) *Patriot-News*, 6 June 1990.

16. Cited in "When the Best Defense Is a Smokescreen" (Viewpoints), *Newsday* 3 May 1990.

17. Richard Mackenzie, "A Conversation with Chuck Horner," *Air Force* 74 (June 1991): 57.

18. David Evans, "From the Gulf," *U.S. Naval Institute Proceedings* 117 (January 1991): 78.

19. So potent was this threat that, in a C-Span interview during a respite from Gulf coverage, Molly Moore of the *Washington Post* became virtually a spokeswoman for the Saudi government, ignoring or playing down the outrageous restrictions the Saudis had imposed on U.S. servicewomen and on the exercise of Christian and Jewish worship by members of the U.S. forces.

20. Georgie Anne Geyer, "Press Brought on Problems with Military, Public," *Harrisburg* (Pa.) *Patriot-News*, 6 March 1991.

21. Richard Harwood, "The Press at War" (Op-Ed), *Washington Post* 10 March 1991.

22. "The decision to quit made itself one evening as I sat in a hotel in Saudi Arabia watching the war, on Cable News Network out of Bahrain. . . . The military hasn't permitted coverage of this war. . . . It has allowed pseudo-coverage—contrived and carefully controlled visits to selected units [by] a few favored outlets (of which I am not one). . . . The press watched itself and made the public think it reported on the war." Fred Reed, "Bowing Out Rather Than Selling Out," *Army Times*, 11 March 1991.

23. Quoted by Lt. Gen. Thomas W. Kelly, "Interview," *U.S. Naval Institute Proceedings* 117 (September 1991): 76.

24. Brent Baker, "Last One in the Pool . . . ," *U.S. Naval Institute Proceedings* 117 (August 1991): 71–72.

25. Bud A. McClure, Letter, *Harrisburg* (Pa.) *Patriot-News*, 26 January 1991.

26. Emogene Trexel "The War News Wasn't News" (Op-Ed), *Harrisburg* (Pa.) *Patriot-News*, 7 March 1991.

27. Alex Jones, "Polls Compare Journalists' and Public Views," *New York Times*, 30 October 1985, p. A13.

28. Quoted in "Editors Told War Coverage Was Thorough," *Portland* (Me.) *Press Herald*, 18 October 1991, p. 4A.

29. Mike Feeley, "4 in News Crew Owe Lives to Tank Leader from Area," *Harrisburg* (Pa.) *Patriot-News*, 1 March 1991, p. 1.

30. Various conversations with the author, 1977–1979.

31. James S. Doyle, correspondence with Newsday, Inc., 13 April 1992.

32. Quoted by Howard Kurtz, "Pulitzer Winner Embroiled in Controversy over Reports," *Washington Post*, 15 April 1992, p. A2.

33. Thomas Griffith, "The Pulitzer Prizes: Giving and Taking Away," *Newsweek* 15 May 1978: "With its clout at Columbia, the *Times* often presses for Pulitzers that

will 'vindicate' its most controversial coverage—the Pentagon Papers, say, or David Halberstam's Vietnam reporting in 1964. This usually works, but Executive Editor Turner Catledge in 1967 sat with tears in his eyes as he learned that the other committee members had overturned Harrison Salisbury's nomination for a wartime journey to Hanoi. ('I was terribly upset,' Catledge wrote, convinced it was a 'decision on political rather than journalistic ground')."

9

Managing the "Right to Lie"

Early on March 2, 1966, the U.S. Department of Defense alerted the Washington press corps that a major announcement would be made at a secretarial press conference later that day.

The briefing room was filled, with overflow connected by intercom in an adjoining room. The reporters were handed one of the most remarkable documents ever released by a government at war—nothing less than the entire troop deployment schedule for U.S. forces being sent to fight in Vietnam, as well as what was available, down to the last battalion, for worldwide contingencies, not least of them a possible Soviet offensive into Western Europe.[1]

"Recently articles have appeared in the press," the announcement began, "which give the impression that because of the major deployments of U.S. military forces to Southeast Asia the United States is now militarily overextended and would not be able to meet other contingencies. . . . "

The recent articles were reports by Hanson W. Baldwin of the *New York Times* that Senate Armed Services Committee investigators had concluded U.S. forces worldwide had, indeed, been gutted to support the deployments to Vietnam. The press conference was designed to refute that charge.

A quick scan of the seven-page, closely typed statement revealed something else: The deployment schedule described could not be achieved without fifteen National Guard divisions that Secretary of Defense Robert S. McNamara had been proclaiming for at least a year to be "excess to military requirements." That was part of an elaborate effort to demonstrate that, while conducting the war in Vietnam, the administration was achieving large savings in overall defense management.

Sitting in front of McNamara as he presented the written statement and invited questions were at least twenty journalists who had heard the description of the Guard divisions as "excess" many times. Surely, someone would ask the secretary about that.

No such thing. As mainly innocuous questions droned on, however, one newsman, not a Pentagon "regular," began to sense that something was wrong. This was Clark Mollenhoff of the Cowles Publications.

Although Mollenhoff could not quite put his finger on the problem initially, it was equally clear that his line of questioning would eventually reveal the contradiction at the heart of the McNamara statement. A couple of questions short of that, McNamara exploded in anger in full view of a national television audience and ordered Mollenhoff out of the room. All the rest of the Washington press corps meekly watched Mollenhoff's dismissal and then resumed the harmless line of questions, making no attempt to pursue the points Mollenhoff had made.[2]

With that incident fresh in mind, Mollenhoff told a college audience a few weeks later, "The daily press is reluctant to take on the job of criticizing those who control the major sources of news at the Pentagon. It is easy to submit to Pentagon news management pressures where the bait is an occasional exclusive story and comfortable, easy access to the 'invitation only background news conferences' with top Pentagon spokesmen. Only a few of the Pentagon reporters will fight the system and risk the cold and uncooperative treatment handed out to those who are regarded as 'unfriendly.' . . . If the daily press does not show the way, magazine writers, columnists and television reporters have difficulty recognizing that a critical problem exists. The work of the courageous few is overwhelmed and inundated by the mass of stories flowing from sycophant journalists who picture the key Pentagon civilians as supermen."[3]

The crucial contradiction regarding the Guard divisions never got into print or on the air. The gutting of U.S. forces worldwide continued, masked by this and other elaborately constructed lies, leading eventually to the "hollow Army" of the 1970s and the enormously costly Reagan administration program to rectify that situation.

More importantly the true cost of the Vietnam War was being withheld from the public, eventually with economic consequences far beyond the defense budget. Out of that grew the "credibility gap" concerning virtually every aspect of the Vietnam War that would eventually destroy Lyndon Johnson's presidency and lead to the most humiliating military defeat the United States has ever suffered.

The groundwork for the control over the press that eventually backfired as the credibility gap began immediately upon accession of the Kennedy administration to power in January 1961. An essential element was the consolidation of Defense Department public affairs authority in the Office of the Assistant Secretary of Defense for Public Affairs, essentially ending the authority of the uniformed services to speak for themselves.[4] Any uniformed officer who might be tempted to violate that arrangement had to consider not only the dismissal of an Army chief of staff and a chief of naval operations for their attempts to warn against policies that ultimately would prove disastrous, but also the actions Attorney General Robert Kennedy had taken in the wake of the disastrous attempt to invade Cuba by proxy at the Bay of Pigs in April 1961.

Although U.S. air crews had been recruited from the Air National Guard to fly B–26s in support of the CIA's Cuban proxies, the Kennedy administration was desperate to keep knowledge of any such direct U.S. involvement from the public. When reports of this involvement began to surface, Robert Kennedy ordered lie-detector-supported interrogations of all of the returned pilots, an act of intimidation that quickly became known throughout the uniformed services.[5]

There have been liars aplenty in all U.S. governments throughout history, but it was in the Kennedy administration that the practice was established and anointed as official policy. That occurred when, boasting of how he had "managed the news" during the Cuban missile crisis of 1962, Arthur Sylvester, assistant secretary of defense for public affairs, proclaimed that the government has a "right to lie" anytime it considers itself to be in a dangerous situation, in particular one in which nuclear war might be possible.

Until his appointment as Pentagon press secretary, Sylvester had spent a lifetime as a newspaper reporter and editor. It is a measure of the contempt for the public held by many professional journalists that it never occurred to Sylvester that it would never be more important to tell the truth to the American public than at a time when nuclear war might be imminent.

The press raised considerable hue and cry about Sylvester's assertion of a "right to lie." But it had already become so deeply identified with the political fortunes of the Kennedy family and the Kennedy appointees in the Pentagon that it dropped the matter when it became apparent that Sylvester had the full backing of Secretary McNamara and of President Kennedy himself.

The prototype of the elaborate deceptions to follow was the very one that gave rise to Sylvester's assertion of a right to lie, the Cuban missile crisis of 1962. Indeed, so successful was that exercise in modern governmental press control that, thirty years later, newspaper editorialists and reporters would continue to assert without doubt or question that the United States and the Soviet Union were on the brink of nuclear war over the emplacement of Soviet missiles in Cuba. Yet the most cursory examination of the overall power relationship available at that time in open sources and certainly known in even greater detail to the Soviet military would show that the Russian homeland would have been devastated in any such war, without comparable damage to the United States. Out of the risk of a few crude and militarily insignificant missiles the Soviets obtained both a guarantee that the United States would not invade Cuba, thus securing Communist dominion of that important outpost, surviving even the demise of Communist power in Russia itself, and the withdrawal of more advanced and militarily significant U.S. missiles then based in Turkey. The United States had sustained a net strategic loss, but through expert press manipulation the Kennedy administration had created an illusion within American journalism that effectively counterbalanced the more obvious Kennedy failures at the Bay of Pigs and in the disastrous Diem episode in Vietnam.[6]

As the TFX affair and a host of lesser programs would demonstrate, once government accepts a "right to lie" as official policy, the lies do not stop with matters of great danger. They become a routine means of doing business, day by day. What was now in progress was the construction of an edifice of information control that would be perfected in the Reagan administration and lead inexorably to such total control of the press in wartime as was achieved throughout the Persian Gulf War of 1991 and the military buildup that preceded it.

Two of the major components of that edifice had existed long before the Kennedy administration had come to power. However, their effectiveness was vastly increased when gathered under the single "tent" erected over military information policies by the Kennedy administration, and when backed by use of the lie detector as an instrument of intimidation.

The military inspector general system had honorable beginnings. The first occupant of that post in the U.S. Army was the remarkable Baron Frederick William Augustus von Steuben. Given total latitude to inspect the Continental Army at Valley Forge and to report directly back to General George Washington, von Steuben put a stop to self-indulgent practices that colonial officers had aped from the artistocratic British officer corps, but that were anathema in the far more democratic Prussian Army, historic stereotypes notwithstanding. From that day forward, U.S. military inspectors general, by whatever title, were intended to enforce adherence to good order and discipline and to make known to senior authority conditions that endangered the good of the service.

Sadly, the system has become in the latter twentieth century a means of protecting senior authority from its own misfeasance and malfeasance and of identifying and punishing those who would dare to challenge or expose such conduct. In this, of course, it is simply following what has become the standard response of American management, civilian as well as military, to any problem: Attack the first person who brings the problem to the attention of management.

Because the military inspectors general are part of the military chain of command, their effectiveness rests solely and entirely on the honesty of the next higher commander. Yet for twenty years following World War II the taxpayer unknowingly, and with the full knowledge of the U.S. Army inspector general system, contributed several million dollars to the establishment and success of a private, profit-making venture, Valley Forge Military Academy at Wayne, Pennsylvania.[7]

The founder of that establishment was one Milton G. Baker who had served as a lieutenant in World War I and who had continued his relationship with the Pennsylvania National Guard thereafter, selling boots to cavalrymen. Having risen in Republican political circles, Baker then obtained an appointment as a "major general" in the Pennsylvania State Guard, a civilian militia organized in the absence of the federalized National Guard during World War II. His last genuine rank had been lieutenant colonel in the U.S. Army Reserve.

By the time the National Guard veterans returned from wartime service, Baker, by then founder and superintendent of Valley Forge Military Academy, was so firmly in control that for at least twenty years thereafter no state adjutant general—the Guard's senior political and military official— would be appointed without Baker's support, in either Republican or Democratic administrations. The reason why eventually came to light when the chief executive officer of Gulf Oil Corporation was forced to resign following the revelation of a $12 million political slush fund, a considerable part of which was channeled through Baker to politicians "on both sides of the aisle."

Out of gratitude, or whatever, Baker's appointees as adjutant general routinely provided to Valley Forge Military Academy some twenty to thirty U.S. Army vehicles, reported as present and accounted for in National Guard motor pools, but, in fact, repainted with the "V.F.M.A." insignia and operating solely for Baker's benefit. These were maintained by federally paid National Guard mechanics and, when worn out, were towed back to the National Guard state maintenance site and replaced by brand new vehicles, all in violation of a federal regulation that prohibited the lending of Army vehicles consigned to the National Guard to any other agency except the Post Office Department and then only for a limited time during the Christmas rush.[8]

Because Valley Forge Military Academy included a two-year junior college with a Reserve Officers' Training Corps (ROTC) program, U.S. Army instructors were permanently assigned at the school, and their office was routinely inspected by representatives of the U.S. Second Army's inspector general at Fort George G. Meade, Maryland. So at least once a year for twenty years U.S. Army inspectors general saw those illegally loaned and illegally repainted U.S. Army vehicles at the school and did nothing to stop the practice.

Baker's political operations had taken him much higher than the state capital. Some considerable part of the Gulf Oil Corporation slush fund went, apparently via Baker, to a U.S. senator from Pennsylvania who, when the fund was revealed, chose not to run for reelection. In deference to that and other channels of influence at the federal level, Baker had been appointed a trustee of the Association of the U.S. Army, the Army's Washington lobby. By now he was wearing the three stars of a lieutenant general, in violation of a federal law prohibiting the wearing of non-federally recognized badges of rank on the federal uniform. Resplendent in his Army blues and three stars, Baker routinely attended Washington banquets in full view of successive inspectors general of the Army, none of whom raised objections.

It was only when Baker let it be known in the late 1960s that he intended to require endorsement by the Republican county chairmen of any promotion to the grade of major and above in the federally paid Pennsylvania National Guard that his control over the Guard and its consequences began to come to public attention. Only when agents of the Federal Bureau of Investigation began looking into the matter were the Army vehicles at Valley Forge returned to public control. The Army made no attempt to recover the millions of dollars the long, illegal subsidy represented. When Baker died, he was accorded a full-page laudatory obituary, with accompanying photograph in his illegal lieutenant general's regalia, in *Army*, the journal of the Association of the U.S. Army.

In Republican-controlled county court houses all over Pennsylvania by that time there were retired Regular Army advisers to the Guard and retired senior members of the Second Army staff serving in comfortable political appointments.

All new members of the services are told that they should report mistreatment or wrongdoing to the local military inspector general. If the inspector general serves an honest commander, an investigation will be made and corrective action taken. If, however, the commander is dishonest, or (as was the case with the Baker affair) if the entire chain of command up to the national level is dishonest, the complainant has walked into a trap. The investigation then will be conducted not with a view toward taking corrective action, but for the purpose of determining the extent of the complainant's knowledge of the situation and the identity of any other likely "threats" to the command.

The general procedure then is to provide the complainant with a report written to "paper over" the matter, with no further action taken. If the complainant is not satisfied to let matters rest there, then he or she has opened a Pandora's box of trouble.

At the end of a long chain of retaliatory administrative actions likely to be taken against the complainant is one that for many years was totally unknown to most members of the service, even many, if not most, of those who retired after a full service career. Any commander or administrative supervisor in the Department of Defense, military or civilian, has the authority to order a subordinate to undergo psychiatric "consultation." Military commanders can order immediate psychiatric confinement.

The psychiatrists to whom military members are consigned are, like the inspectors general, under the military chain of command. They know that when a patient is ordered by a superior officer to appear for "consultation," such is expected to result in a finding that the person is in some way unstable.

On January 31, 1983, CBS's "60 Minutes" reported several cases in which members of the U.S. Air Force had been confined in psychiatric wards for having reported, among other things, infractions of flying safety. In response to that broadcast and to numerous other fully documented reports of military psychiatric abuse, the American Psychiatric Association appointed a committee to report on such abuses and to develop a code of conduct for military psychiatrists faced with such demands for unethical conduct. The committee recommended procedures that would have given both the patient and the doctor at least some protection against abuse. Military psychiatrists blocked approval of the report.[9] Then Representative Barbara Boxer (D–Calif.) introduced legislation designed to correct the abuses, but it has been blocked by the Department of Defense.

During the same period, the U.S. government and the American Psychiatric Association were exerting international pressure to force the then Soviet government to stop using forced psychiatric "consultation" and confinement as punishment for political dissidents. That practice was outlawed by the governments that succeeded the Soviet Union. It remains a standard method of suppressing dissent and reports of waste, fraud, corruption, and mismanagement in the U.S. government, in particular the U.S. Department of Defense and the armed forces.

Among the internal information control features introduced in the Department of Defense by the Kennedy administration and employed ever since is a requirement that press contact with any senior official be monitored by a public relations officer who must report ultimately to the political leadership of the department. At various times periodic written reports have also been required as a means of divulging any press contacts that escaped the monitoring process. During the Persian Gulf buildup and war of 1990–91, this system of monitoring was extended to the battlefield, whereby every reporter had to be accompanied by a press officer, all conversations with military personnel monitored by the press officers (many of them as ignorant of military operations as the reporters), and all written and photographic reports resulting from such contacts transmitted only after military review and approval.

This went far beyond the system of formal censorship that had been in effect during World War II when correspondents were free to talk with whomever they wished without a monitor; their copy was subject to review before transmittal, but only for very specific operational infractions. As employed in the Persian Gulf War, military monitors interfered on grounds of "rudeness" to prevent transmittal of information that might prove embarrassing to individuals or the service—as when Navy pilots were found to be watching a pornographic movie in the ready room—and because "the general didn't like your last story."[10]

When not under the extreme pressures of war, defense "management" of the news is usually much more sophisticated. One of the most important documents published by the Defense Department is "Current News," a daily compilation of every defense-related story that appeared in the national and major regional press, including radio and television, the previous day. Journalists identified by this and other means as politically supportive of the administration, or just generally sympathetic with the current defense program, are invited in for "backgrounders," a process that has deeply corrupted the entire flow of information from the government to the public. By this means the press is engaged to transmit to the public without identification as to the source, information and, at least as often, innuendo and outright lies designed to support a program with which the source does not wish to be identified, undermine an opponent, or float a "trial balloon" (i.e., an idea that can be abandoned if it proves to be too controversial). The process reached its ultimate in the adaptation to print by Bob Woodward of the *Washington Post*, in such books as *The Commanders*, of the mixture of fact and fiction known to television as the "docu-drama."

The basis for the entire control edifice, of course, is the system of "classification" by which documents are marked "Confidential," "Secret," or "Top Secret," determined supposedly by the degree of damage to the national security interest that would be incurred if the information were to become public. The system has no direct basis in law. It has been established and is conducted entirely by executive order.

While varying attempts have been made to control the number of people authorized to classify a document, no one ever has been punished for overclassifying a document. Thus, literally millions of documents have been improperly classified, each of them imposing an economic penalty in terms of accountability, security, and formally recorded destruction or review for eventual public release. All who have handled such documents, including Reagan administration officials who undertook the most extreme measures to date to protect them, admit that the system has been grossly abused, at enormous cost to the taxpayer.[11]

There are other costs, potentially far more damaging to the national interest.

In 1964, then Secretary of Defense Robert McNamara attempted to resolve a costly, age-old problem by merging the federally run and state-run military reserve systems into a single, common-sense whole. A brigadier general and two colonels were sequestered in a small office, armed with authority to classify anything and everything and told to come up with a plan. They did, and it almost worked. But as Regular officers, none of the three understood that their proposed solution would expose members of the federal forces to state political patronage by placing them under the control of state politicians, the adjutants general who operate the National Guard system on behalf of the governors.

Had it not been for the secrecy in which the plan was evolved, the planners would have been forced to confront that issue much sooner, and a solution—require separation of the military and political functions as at the federal level—would have been readily discovered. As it was, it was not until the plan was presented to Congress that the failure to assure protection from state political patronage was revealed. Opponents of the plan, intent on preserving their own sinecures, leaped on the weakness, with fatal results.

During the decades since, that failure has cost the taxpayer billions of dollars in duplicative facilities and services. Worse, it has perpetuated an antique and inadequate system, in particular in the Army, that failed once again during the Persian Gulf War to provide a reliable system of timely replacement and reinforcement for deployed Regular combat units.

All successful modern human enterprises operate on the understanding that maximum exchange of information is the key not only to success, but also to survival. Politics and the military—potentially the most dangerous of all human activities—operate on precisely the opposite principle.

The pace of change in all modern human endeavors is such that the sequestering of information for whatever reason ensures that it will be quickly made obsolete by isolation from new ideas and new developments. That is true of most of the classified information expensively locked away within the U.S. government, in particular the Department of Defense and the military services. The Defense Department compounds that problem by a system of prepublication "security reviews" that have nothing to do with security and everything to do with maintaining undeviating support for the "party line" of whatever political administration happens to be in power.

In 1982 Reagan administration Deputy Secretary of Defense Frank Carlucci initiated the most restrictive prepublication review policies in the history of the Defense Department.[12] Although the directive by which he executed that policy contains the usual kudos to "security," the operative requirement was that "Material submitted in compliance with the requirements of this Directive shall be cleared for public release only [if] it is consistent with established . . . policies and programs."

So thoroughly did Carlucci stifle professional debate within the military services that one of the most important forums for such discussion, the *Air University Review*, the professional journal of the senior Air Force service schools, was forced to cease publication. It was succeeded by a journal, whose "stated purpose was to focus on 'warfighting,' "—safely beyond any subject area that would bring into question "policies and programs."[13]

Alarmed at this suffocation of professional dialogue, the Navy took unusually bold action by publishing a long series of attacks on the prepublication review system in the privately published U.S. *Naval Institute Proceedings*.

From these carefully written articles and comments, extending from June 1990 through June 1991, it became apparent that one of the principal means of throttling meaningful professional discourse within and between the services was to delay manuscripts in the "security review" process until they were no longer relevant.

"All competent naval professionals know intuitively where the lines are drawn to define material as a 'security violation,' " Commander Bruce Linder wrote in the August 1990 *Proceedings*. "This is drilled into people with regularity. Less distinct are the lines that define currently correct 'policy.' However, I have found that these 'policy' questions are almost always self-enforcing. If an author is so far off-base as not to have checked current policy, then it is doubtful that his work will have sufficient merit to clear normal editorial review. If it somehow passes the editors but is still wide of the mark, it is sure to be scorched in subsequent comments from knowledgeable readers. We should never allow 'policy' restrictions to thwart responsible discussion of alternative means to an end or to uncover deficiencies, defects, or artless tunnel-vision."[14]

Bitter over being forced by outraged public opinion to give up large payments for speeches that were ill-disguised bribes, Congress compounded the prepublication review process by denying service members the few hundred dollars the professional service journals pay for professional articles. That, however, has been ruled unconstitutional by the courts, as an infringement of First Amendment rights. It is still not clear, however, that service members may accept payment for articles directly related to their own duties. Only token, in terms of monetary reward, such payment offers an important incentive to the effort involved over and above normal duty.

Both the press and the public have an important stake in ending the prepublication restrictions. The open professional debate by authoritative authors thus made possible is a vital element of the public's understanding of complex national security issues, all the more so because American journalism refuses to train and support competent specialists in defense coverage.

Not all administrations make full use of the apparatus for control and distortion of public information.

During the 1977 presidential campaign, then candidate James E. Carter called for withdrawal of all remaining U.S. military units in South Korea. On the day of his inauguration, President Carter summoned the Joint Chiefs of Staff and apparently confirmed that the troop withdrawal was to be executed.

Within an hour after Army Chief of Staff Bernard W. Rogers returned to the Pentagon from that conference, L. James Binder, editor of *Army* magazine, called a civilian Asian specialist who was then on military Reserve duty in the Pentagon and asked if he could prepare an article setting forth the reasons why withdrawal of the U.S. forces would not be a good idea. The article was written even as the Carter inaugural balls were in progress.

The March issue of the magazine was recalled from the printer and the article opposing troop withdrawal inserted as the lead and cover story.[15]

Immediately upon publication, the *Army* article was brought to the attention of an Atlanta attorney with close ties both to Mr. Carter and to the *Atlanta Journal and Constitution*. Joseph Minter, editorial page director, asked the author of the *Army* article to write a summary as part of a "pro and con" debate. When the White House was asked to provide the "pro" argument, the only public official who could be found who would take on the job was Senator George McGovern of North Dakota, leader of the extreme liberal faction of the Democratic party, from which Carter had distanced himself.[16]

What that said when the debate appeared in print was that the Carter administration had begun to back off from the troop withdrawal decision. Indeed, the issue had sent shudders throughout an Asia fearful that U.S. withdrawal would provide a murderous North Korean regime with what may well have been its last chance to drag China and the Soviet Union into a final attempt to conquer South Korea, very possibly triggering a world war.

The Carter administration made no attempt to retaliate against General Rogers or the Reserve officer and civilian Army employee who were fighting the Korea troop withdrawal idea, in close alliance with General (Retired) Richard G. Stilwell, a former United Nations commander in Korea. Stilwell, was orchestrating opposition from civilian academics and the governments of Japan, South Korea, Taiwan, and Singapore, with surreptitious agreement from China and the Soviet Union, both deeply worried about being drawn into a war for which they had no stomach.

Eventually, the troop withdrawal idea was quietly buried.

By permitting a full public debate of the issue the Carter administration had saved itself, and possibly the world, from a disaster.

Given the damage done by exercising the claimed "right to lie" in the TFX episode, in the creation of the Vietnam credibility gap, and in the Iran-Contra controversy that afflicted the administration of President Ronald Reagan, it would seem obvious that, moral considerations aside, no democratic government can benefit ultimately from use of these elaborate processes of suppression and distortion. Yet many of the same people who participated in the open debate of the Korean troop withdrawal issue during the Carter administration, and saw its benefits, acted as members of the Reagan administration to vastly expand prepublication review and use of the lie detector to suppress debate to an extent never before practiced.

Ironically, the press, which cheered on many of the practices by which information and thought control were developed to a fine art during the Kennedy administration, completely misinterpreted the ultimate impact of the process. In the aftermath of the Vietnam War, the press was convinced that it would never again be possible, in the face of modern television technology, for governments to mislead the public in matters of war and peace. Indeed, there was an active debate for a time among prominent national journalists as to whether a major war could ever again be possible in the face of such media technology. Yet from the moment the president decided to intervene until the last shot was fired, the Persian Gulf War of 1990–91 would prove to be the first war in U.S. history in which the press was so totally controlled that there would never be a timely public or congressional questioning of the presidential decisions that committed the country irrevocably to what could have been a nuclear war.

To anyone who truly values the democratic concept that must be a source of deep concern.

NOTES

1. U.S. Department of Defense, Office of the Assistant Secretary of Defense for Public Affairs, "Statement of Secretary of Defense Robert S. McNamara" (News Release), 2 March 1966.

2. The degree of control McNamara had achieved over the press can be judged from the more normal, and professional, reaction of news reporters when hotelier and tax-evader Leona Helmsley attempted to bar a reporter from the New York Post from a news conference: "Alex Michelini, a reporter for The Daily News, went to the press room and suggested to other reporters that they walk out, which they did." "Chronicle," New York Times, 20 September 1991, p. B6.

3. Clark R. Mollenhoff, Address at Iowa Wesleyan College, Mt. Pleasant, Iowa, 28 May 1966. Reprinted in the Congressional Record, 11 October 1966.

4. "Further limiting the independence of the press are orders [by which] the functions of the Army, Navy and Air Force information offices are being cut back and the information centralized in the Office of the Assistant Secretary, Arthur Sylvester." Clark R. Mollenhoff, in The Press in Washington ed. Ray Eldon Hiebert (New York: Dodd, Mead & Co., 1967) 214.

5. This description was given to the author by one of the pilots who participated in the Bay of Pigs support operations, Lieutenant Colonel James C. Elliott, Virginia Air National Guard.

6. There were a few in the press who understood the dimensions of what the Kennedy administration was creating. "Mr. Kennedy," former New York Times Washington Bureau chief Arthur Krock wrote in the March 1963 issue of Fortune magazine, "prefers the intimate background briefings of journalists, and their publishers, on a large scale, from which [they] emerge in a state of protracted enchantment. . . . The "informational directives' prescribed for the Pentagon" inflate success or gloss over error "in the aftermath of half-won showdowns—such as President Kennedy's with respect to the Soviet rearmament of Cuba." Quoted in Associated Press, "Newsman Accuses JFK of Cynicism in News Handling," Harrisburg (Pa.) Patriot-News, 24 April 1963.

7. Ben A. Franklin and Hanson W. Baldwin in companion articles, the New York Times, 27 April 1967, p. 1.

8. The beneficiaries of such largesse are never quite content. According to Lieutenant Colonel George Kuhn, then assistant state maintenance officer of the Pennsylvania National Guard, Baker decided that none of the government vehicles on

hand was quite good enough to permit the late Francis Cardinal Spellman of New York to conduct a mounted review of the Valley Forge corps of cadets. So Baker ordered the Guard to supply a brand new jeep; he then had the wheels chromed and a large chrome star affixed to the hood. Even Baker was uncomfortable with keeping that visible to the Army inspectors on campus, so he had it returned to the Guard at its Fort Indiantown Gap headquarters immediately after the review. The Guard, however, was now faced with a quandary. Up to then it had managed to avoid creating the self-incriminating "paper trail" that some honest inspector general might someday stumble across. To reconvert the spruced-up jeep to Army standard, however, would require a work order, and the dreaded paper trail would be started. The solution was to lock the jeep up in a shed behind the maintenance shop where it may rest to the present day. On many winter evenings, gazing into the firelight, I have pictured Cardinal Spellman riding in that jeep, the picture displayed on page one of the *New York Daily News*. "Hmmm," James Weighart, Washington bureau chief and later editor of the *Daily News*, responded when I related that never-to-be-realized dream, "Cardinal Spellman in a hot jeep. Yeah, I think they would have used it."

9. Author's discussions with Dr. R. Dale Walker, chairman of the American Psychiatric Association's Committee on the Abuse and Misuse of Psychiatry in the U.S., 1988–89. According to Dr. Walker, a report by his committee effectively condemning the use of psychiatry to punish military whistleblowers was to be presented to the association's board of governors for final approval in September 1989. The association did not act on the report, apparently through the influence of military psychiatrists, who are members of the association.

10. R. W. Apple, Jr., "Correspondents Protest Pool System," *New York Times*, 12 February 1991, p. A14.

11. Edwin Meese, the Reagan administration attorney general, once described the system as producing a "ho-hum attitude toward security."

12. U.S. Department of Defense, Office of the Secretary of Defense, Department of Defense Directive 5230.9, "Clearance of DoD Information for Public Release," 2 April 1982.

13. G. Murphy Donovan, "Strategic Literacy," *Airpower Journal* (Winter 1988): 72.

14. Bruce Lender, "Comment and Discussion," *U.S. Naval Institute Proceedings* 116 (August 1990): 16.

15. William V. Kennedy, "Yankee, Don't Go Home," *Army* 27 (March 1977): 14–18.

16. George McGovern and William V. Kennedy, "The Issue: Korea" *Atlanta Journal and Constitution*, (Weekend People & Opinion), 11 June 1977, p. 1-B.

10

How to Defeat the "Right to Lie"

Back at the Plaza Hotel in New York after a nationwide tour in the early 1950s, Hildegarde, the incomparable chanteuse of that era and several others, observed that "There are no more provinces."

With every year of the decades since, Atlanta, Pittsburgh, Chicago, Milwaukee, New Orleans, Denver, Seattle, San Francisco, and Los Angeles have acquired more and more of the international character of the old northeastern U.S. ports. By at least 1965 each of them was targeted for instantaneous destruction by intercontinental ballistic missiles. By at least 1990 the economic welfare of each of them depended on the ability to compete in the international marketplace.

Why, then, do their newspapers go on behaving as though each is still primarily the urban center of a surrounding agricultural or industrial region that draws its strength solely from the domestic U.S. market and its safety from the Atlantic and Pacific oceans?

Not one of them has assigned to coverage of national and international security affairs a journalist trained—as a journalist—for that role. Not one of them has maintained a full-time research assistant with the budgetary support needed to free the national security writer and analyst from domination by the daily Pentagon handouts. All have left the field of national security reporting and analysis primarily to the *New York Times* and the *Wall Street Journal*, as though such concerns enter the country only by means of the latest ship from Europe to dock at a North River pier.

Since television news and, to a slightly lesser extent, the weekly news magazines depend solely and entirely on what their staffs read in the daily newspaper, the American public at large is also at the mercy of two very fallible newspapers, each severely restricted by its own ideological bent and regional or economic focus.

Neither of the major New York newspapers has ever informed its readers that, had Iraq been able to explode a single experimental nuclear device at the moment its army raced into Kuwait during the first week of August 1990, the entire strategic situation would have changed. Even without proof that Iraq was capable of delivering a nuclear weapon—or, indeed, possessed anything beyond the exploded experimental device—no major allied naval task force could have been risked in the confined waters of the Persian Gulf. Certainly, no Marine amphibious task force with its thousands of men and dozens of ships could have been employed in the gulf. The concentration of large numbers of allied aircraft at a few Saudi air bases would have been out of the question. The method of inserting troops and equipment into the country would have had to be changed entirely to avoid the enormous congestion that in fact occurred because of freedom from a nuclear threat. Instead of the few huge logistics installations that were created to serve the allied armies, hundreds of smaller bases would have been required, adding months to the buildup process.

Indeed, it would have been necessary for the United States and its allies to reconsider the whole question of whether and how to challenge the Iraqi occupation of Kuwait. Saudi Arabia may well have decided right off that the risks were too high and that an arrangement short of war had to be made with Iraq.

The lesson has not been lost. Every government on earth understands by now that to possess, or at least to be allied with a power that possesses, even one nuclear weapon is to be treated with respect in the councils of the mighty. To be without nuclear weapons is to be acted upon. With some twenty nations already in possession of nuclear weapons or well on the way to acquiring them, non-proliferation is a myth.

Not only have the *New York Times* and the *Wall Street Journal* failed to alert their readers to the implications of this, but also they have lulled the reader into thinking that the danger of nuclear war ended with the distintegration of the Soviet Union. That was done deliberately in the case of the *New York Times* in order to support its ideological position on the defense budget and by omission on the part of a *Wall Street Journal* dedicated to the proposition that all of human activity beyond the stock market is of peripheral concern.

Neither newspaper has ever made an attempt to cover on a meaningful, continuing basis the two institutions upon which the long-term stability of the emerging international economic community depends—the Japanese armed forces and the German army.

Do the ghosts of the Imperial Japanese Army and the old Prussian mindset remain to be awakened and take charge again in some future crisis? In supporting the U.S. government's opposition to a mainly Franco-German

European army are the editorialists helping to drive Germany back into the fortress mentality that led to two world wars?

Never once has either the *Times* or the *Journal* alerted its readers to the crucial role Taiwan plays in Japanese strategic thinking. The reporters they have sent to Japan have uniformly demonstrated the repugnance and, indeed, the contempt of American journalists for anything to do with the military. Had they behaved otherwise, they might have learned that Taiwan is second only to Korea in terms of strategic importance to Japan and that extension of mainland Chinese control to the island could set in motion the process by which the world will see some forty Japanese "boomers" (nuclear submarines equipped with nuclear-armed intercontinental ballistic missiles) deployed throughout the world's oceans.

One might think these intriguing story possibilities. Not to the *Times* or the *Journal*, and, therefore, not to the rest of American journalism.

The press does not bear the full, or even the principal, burden for this failure to tell the public that it is entering a world fully as dangerous, albeit in different ways, as the one it knew during the Cold War. The principal agency that the public created to do that job is the U.S. Government. Yet the U.S. government as it presently operates deliberately seeks to exclude the public and to retain power over all major decisions within a narrow self-appointed elite. It does that by maintaining its self-defeating policies of deliberately lying and suppressing public dialogue by military and civilian officials trained at vast public expense to discuss such matters, and by intimidating and punishing honest employees seeking to expose and correct wrongdoing.

Much of the responsibility for this situation lies with Congress. Congress has failed to provide a carefully defined legislative framework—or any framework at all—for control of classified information.

In an address to the U.S. Army Armor Association in May 1977 General William E. DePuy, then commanding general of the U.S. Army Training and Doctrine Command, warned that "There are no secrets about warfare: there are maybe just a few little technical secrets such as the inside of a thermalsight [night vision device] or details of how a diode works. But they are probably the only secrets left."[1]

In the years since DePuy made that speech the availability of satellite photographs and other imagery from international commercial sources and the rapid technical advances in computer science have further eroded whatever basis there once was for large-scale classification. Yet, during a three-year period between 1983 and 1985, reflecting the Reagan administration's obsession with secrecy, the number of documents classified each year grew from 17 million to 22 million.[2] There are now some one trillion classified documents, all supposedly of such importance that the publication of any one of them would endanger the national security of the United States.

Even as the Reagan administration was filling up this huge and enormously expensive warehouse of secrecy, its attorney general, Edwin Meese III, acknowledged that "We have far too much classified information in the Federal Government. A lot of things which shouldn't be classified are, and therefore there is a kind of ho-hum attitude toward the protection of national security information."[3]

"Secrecy," in the view of Edward Teller, the nuclear scientist, "does not lead to security. . . . Secrecy makes it impossible for a large part of the community of scientists even to come in contact with problems related to defense work. Discussion can be carried out only among those who have clearance, but many scientists choose not to obtain clearance because of the complications and restrictions it imposes. Only those who have exceptionally high clearance ratings can consider the newest and most difficult questions. Such people are few in number and exceptionally busy. This means that progress on the most important questions will be slow and may contain errors. The driving force of scientific work—widespread consideration and collaboration by well motivated individuals—is absent on the most important questions."[4]

What Teller said of science can be said with at least equal force about all other aspects of defense planning from politics and geography to organization and training.

Not only did the classified swamp continue to expand under the Reagan and Bush administrations, but also it began to move ever closer to the point of dragging down journalists and others outside the government.

Although Congress has failed to define what can and cannot be classified, it has enacted legislation that permits the executive branch to prosecute people for disclosure of information that the executive branch classifies solely on its own authority.

In 1985 Samuel Loring Morison, a naval intelligence analyst, was prosecuted and convicted for having sold to a British publication, for which he was a "stringer," what the U.S. government claimed to be a properly classified photograph.

Strangely, the *New York Times* argued in an editorial that there is somehow a distinction between unauthorized delivery of classified information to a publication, U.S. or foreign, and unauthorized delivery to a foreign government.[5] In the peculiar logic that has become the hallmark of *Times* editorials, nothing was said of the fact that, whatever the motivation, the ultimate result was revelation to its enemies of information that supposedly would endanger the United States.

In this and other cases the courts reached the common-sense conclusion that the crime is in the disclosure.

Establishment of the principle that the guilt is in the disclosure will lead inevitably to prosecution of journalists who have received classified documents by one means or another, who fail to return the documents immediately upon receipt, and who compound the act by publishing the classified information. Given the post-Vietnam record of public support for the government in matters of national security, prosecution could result in conviction, especially in a period of danger. In that event grave damage will have been done to the First Amendment. In effect, the United States will have stumbled into an Official Secrets Act on the British model whereby the government can conceal anything deemed to be a matter of "national security." As has long been demonstrated in Britain, that means anything politicians in charge, and the upper-class establishment in general, deem to be embarrassing.

The anomaly of the Reagan administration attorney general and a prominent pro-Reagan scientist arguing for reduction in government secrecy while the same administration was moving both to expand secrecy to unprecedented proportions and to use every legal and quasi-legal form of intimidation to punish real or perceived infractions testifies to the inability of the executive branch to gain control of the classification monster. Secrecy offers far too many advantages to the inadequate, the incompetent, and the corrupt administrator to be surrendered voluntarily.

If there is to be corrective action before the present trend leads to permanent damage both to the First Amendment and to the true national security interest, it must come from Congress, and it must be bold action indeed.

The categories of information for which there is a legitimate need for secrecy are few and easily defined:

- Codes and code-breaking technology
- Intelligence files that would reveal ongoing operations and U.S. agents and sources
- Military operations in time of war, or at other times when American lives are immediately at risk
- Specific performance data of weapons and weapons delivery systems prior to deployment (after which photography, other sensors, and expert analysis thereof reveal virtually all data)

No other categories of information can be said to threaten the safety of individual citizens or the nation. There are personnel, investigative, and contractual matters that require confidentiality, but not under national security markings and laws.

That means that security markings could be removed from upwards of 90 percent of the classified information now held by the U.S. government. The immediate fiscal savings would be in the hundreds of millions of dollars. The improvement in terms of overall efficiency would be almost infinitely great, for all the reasons cited by Dr. Teller.

Any such legislation should provide severe penalties *both* for unauthorized release of legitimately classified information to anyone and for misuse of classification authority to conceal misconduct. As was pointed out in the most comprehensive congressional examination of the subject to date, failure of

Congress to legislate penalties for misuse of the classification system is one of the primary causes of its abuse.[6]

Given a classification system in which all parties concerned could have faith, the press would properly be subject to criminal prosecution if it were to obtain or accept such information beyond the proper channels for declassification and release. Public officials who make selective release of classified information—now a common practice—to bolster credibility in "background" briefings should also be subject to severe penalties.

All of what the public learns of national defense comes from some source within the defense establishment itself. The Orwellian system of controls established in the Kennedy administration and brought to fruition in the Reagan administration is designed to assure that the public will learn only what the political administration in control wants it to learn—the entire history of the Persian Gulf War being a model of what can be expected unless drastic changes are made.

Elimination of the fraudulent prepublication security review process is, therefore, every bit as essential as reform of the classification system. Once secrecy is limited to its legitimate proportions, the areas of genuinely classified information will be small enough to be controlled at the source. That is, everyone who is granted access to such information will clearly understand its nature and the penalties for unauthorized release. These legitimate controls would be sufficient to preclude inadvertent use in published material. Whatever small risk of disclosure would remain would be a small price to pay to gain the intellectual benefits described by Dr. Teller. Indeed, it is no exaggeration to state that no nation will be able to survive as a major power in the intensely competitive world that is emerging unless it is a full participant in that intellectual process.

Given the burden of original sin, no human activity will be free of error and corruption. The inspector general system was supposed to take that into account, but it has been made into a means of protecting the status quo and the inadequacies, and worse, of command.

The minimal action needed to correct this situation is removal of military inspectors general from the military chain of command. But if they are only to be concentrated under the political control of the secretary of defense and the administration he or she serves, nothing will have been accomplished. What is needed is an inspector general of the United States reporting solely to Congress, as do the directors of the Library of Congress and the General Accounting office. Within each department of government, civilian or military, inspectors general should continue to operate as at present, but they should be independent of the administrative structures they are intended to police. The basic principle here is that no human activity can be trusted to police itself.

It is equally important that the military medical services be removed from the military, and the Department of Defense, chain of command. Only by such means can the present practice of using compliant military psychiatrists as the last defense of the corrupt and incompetent military commander be eradicated.

A neurologist is a neurologist, and a nurse is a nurse, whether he or she works with the Army, Navy, Air Force, or Marine Corps. Some degree of specialized training is required to enable the medical professional to operate within and respond to the particular service environment, but nothing so fundamental that permanent assignment to a particular service is required. Indeed, the Navy medical corps already operates across the entire defense environment from flight medicine to Marine Corps field hospitals, all personnel being interchangeable. It would be only a short, common-sense step beyond that to assignment of all government medical personnel to the Public Health Service, with detail to the military as required. Those detailed to a particular military service could wear the uniform of that service without being subject to the illegitimate administrative pressures that have perverted military psychiatry.

While the administrative reforms cited would largely open up national defense to public view, that view would continue to be obscured by a press that, except for a tiny handful of its members, lacks the training, time, and means to make sense of the information available in a timely and meaningful manner.[7]

First and foremost, American journalism must escape from the tyranny of the *New York Times*. It is absurd that the whims and prejudices of a single family should dominate the attitudes of the national press, print and broadcast, to the extent that is documented by every major study ever undertaken of the subject.

As the ideological content of *Times*'s defense reporting has increased from 1963 onward, the reliability of that reporting has declined. Having destroyed, for ideological reasons, the center for defense reporting and analysis built up by A. H. Sulzberger and Adolph Ochs Adler, the editors responsible—principally A. M. Rosenthal and his successor, Max Frankel—were never able to develop a satisfactory substitute. No reporter and analyst could be found who could reconcile the newspaper's Vietnam and post-Vietnam anti-military ideology with honest reporting and analysis of the military story. The *Times*'s defense coverage of the 1930s through the 1950s remains, however, the model on which comprehensive, competent defense coverage can be rebuilt.

If the *Philadelphia Inquirer*, the *Atlanta Journal and Constitution*, the *Los Angeles Times*, and the other major regional newspapers can assure expert coverage of the local police and fire departments, there is far more reason why they should be providing coverage at least as expert in the national and international security field.

Only a relatively few people are affected by crime and the normal run of urban fires. The lives and the economic well-being of every person in those

communities and regions are at stake every minute of the day in a world
threatened by nuclear-armed chaos.

A trained military specialist in the Pentagon newsroom, operating in close
cooperation with a military editor in the home office, both backed by competent, full-time research assistance, is the minimum requirement for any
enterprise, print or broadcast, that claims to be a major regional or national
journalistic institution.

That still leaves the largest single gap in current defense reporting—
coverage of the major U.S. and allied military commands. Since no thought
would ever be given to diverting resources from the sports department, that
is beyond the economic resources of any one major newspaper or network.

What is needed is a military bureau within the AP's New York headquarters. Such a bureau should have control of AP Pentagon coverage, and
it should have correspondents assigned, full-time, to each of the major U.S.
joint military commands—Atlantic, Pacific, Strategic, and so on—plus the
North Atlantic Treaty Organization in Brussels and the senior U.S. commands in Japan and Korea, at least for as long as major deployments of U.S.
forces remain overseas. The normal career pattern of those correspondents
should be five years at a major command and five years in Washington. The
New York office should have a research staff adequate to keep track of the
specialized military press and academic sources, American and foreign.

The principal function of the New York office should be to support the
deployed correspondents and to provide expert editing and direction. Never
again should it be possible for a distorted "first report" of enemy action to
be transmitted directly to the public without experienced assessment and
evaluation, as was done by Peter Arnett of the AP and Walter Cronkite of
CBS News during the Tet Offensive, with disastrous results for genuine U.S.
security interests.

There are enough readily identifiable American journalists who have demonstrated a talent and a desire to cover military affairs to begin operation of
such a bureau immediately. For those and all future correspondents and
researchers, to include those working for newspapers and, however remote
the possibility, the networks, there should be a methodical, ongoing program
of training.

The only positive development in defense coverage over the past thirty
years has been the emergence of the Center for Defense Journalism at Boston
University. At some point, probably at the completion of the initial tour at
a major command, the military specialist should be sent at his or her employer's expense to complete a graduate course under the direction of the
Center for Defense Journalism or the equivalent in other universities. The
principal elements of the military Command and General Staff College correspondence course should be integrated into the curriculum.

It would be a simple matter, given adequate funding, for such a center to set up short introductory courses that would give newly hired military correspondents a grounding in the defense field.

Once the press has created such a corps of trained defense specialists, it will be difficult or impossible for the Department of Defense to deny at least the assigned AP reporter at a major command continued access to that command in time of war or other military emergency, to include deployment with the command headquarters. The public would then be assured of knowledgeable, independent reporting from the first moment of a military operation, subject to reasonable military censorship.

Beyond the first twenty-four hours or so of initial deployment a pool arrangement of some sort must be substituted for the absurd mass of ill-informed genuine, quasi-genuine, and outright fake journalists who have plagued every U.S. military operation since Vietnam.[8] The degree of public support for the limitation of press operations in time of war, demonstrated in every major military operation since Grenada, is such that the only question to be resolved is whether such pools are to be run by the government or by the press. So long as the press refuses to employ and train competent defense specialists, the government is within its rights to control such pools as closely as was done during the Persian Gulf War.

Once U.S. military forces are committed to a post of danger, their safety and success are paramount. The press can operate freely in such an environment only to the extent that it can assure the American public that its agents have the degree of loyalty, training, and demonstrated competence necessary to be trusted outside of close military supervision. Such was not the case in Vietnam, nor in the Persian Gulf War.

American journalism is faced with a truly daunting task in regaining the trust of the American public, lost through the incompetent reporting that occurred during the Vietnam War, and that was demonstrated beyond any doubt by the journalists in the televised press conferences during the Persian Gulf War.

The first requirement to be met in restoring that trust is to assure that all persons hired by the American press to cover U.S. forces in peace or war will be U.S. citizens. Only years after the war was it discovered that a principal Vietnamese staff member of CBS in Saigon was a Viet Cong agent.[9] Plainly, any background information given to CBS correspondents by the U.S. military during the course of the war and discussed in the supposed privacy of the CBS Saigon bureau was channeled straight to the enemy. The Saigon bureaus of all other major American news organizations were similarly dependent on foreign nationals. To suppose that CBS was the only victim of successful enemy penetration would be naive.

Even where there is no outright subversion, the employment of journalists and staff members with no legal or emotional attachment to the United States leads inevitably to the subordination of U.S. interests and armed forces security to the interests of whatever governments or ideologies the foreign nationals serve.

No doubt about it—to demand citizenship as a fundamental element of trust repudiates the notion that the journalist is only an observer and reporter, rather than a participant who shares responsibility for the outcome of the events observed and reported.

Were David Halberstam, Neil Sheehan, and Peter Arnett mere observers of the events that led to the overthrow and murder of President Ngo Dinh Diem of South Vietnam and the irredeemable political chaos that followed? Not only were they participants, but also, at least for a time, they exulted in that role and were praised for it by such as James Reston, William Small, and others among American journalism's most influential and respected senior managers.

Were Peter Arnett, then of AP, and Walter Cronkite of CBS, then the nation's most respected television news anchor, mere reporters, or were they participants when they reported to the nation an entirely erroneous impression of the success achieved by Communist infiltrators during the 1968 Tet Offensive? Their reporting helped to break the will of a U.S. president and his principal subordinates. It would be difficult to define "participation" in any stronger terms.

Every word the journalist writes or broadcasts concerning an event is a form of participation in that event, with profound effects on the ultimate outcome. The only question that remains is whether the journalist is competent to be trusted with such power.

As was demonstrated by the televised press conferences during the Persian Gulf War, journalists, with only rare exceptions, are the least competent of all participants in current U.S. military operations.

All of the military officers who participated in those briefings, from the lowest rank to the highest, were the products of extensive training beyond the college level tailored to his or her particular grade and assignment. The same was true of all other professional groups operating within the military establishment and present in that theater of operations. A doctor who is trained as a general practitioner is not permitted to perform open heart surgery. A registered nurse cannot perform anesthesiology without extensive advanced training. A flight engineer on a transport aircraft is not permitted to fly as copilot. From bulldozer operator to general, every member of the Army Corps of Engineers present had received intensive, specialized training commensurate with his or her level of responsibility.

The only profession other than journalism that claims universal competence on the basis of entry-level training is the legal profession. The result is that innocent and unknowing clients are victimized every day by lawyers operating beyond their depth and unwilling to admit it. Lawyers, at least, must complete a level of training beyond college. Not so journalists, a liberal arts or journalism baccalaureate degree being considered license to cover with competence anything from the election of a pope to nuclear war. Even the advanced degrees usually acquired by journalists have little or no relevance to such specialized fields as national defense, business, religion, health, engineering, and so on because they are often in such amorphous areas as political "science" and journalism itself.

Editors, publishers, and broadcasters have fought the growing demand for highly trained specialists on the basis of the claim that such specialists tend to become identified with their sources, or that they became too narrow in outlook.[10]

Yet identification with the national security interests of the United States and with the safety and success of its armed forces is precisely what the American public is demanding. Nothing, however, in those powerfully expressed attitudes suggests that the public is demanding an uncritical relationship.

The lonely effort by Hanson W. Baldwin and a handful of other military specialists from 1961 onwards to warn that Kennedy administration appointees in the Department of Defense were leading the country into a potential disaster, while the great majority of American editorialists and broadcasters were making virtual demigods out of those same appointees, makes the argument of excessive identification absurd. It was the specialists who were critical of a Defense leadership headed for disaster. It was the generalists who identified themselves so closely with that leadership that the warning was suppressed.

The profound ignorance demonstrated over national and international television by the majority of journalists assigned to cover the Persian Gulf War demonstrated that such ignorance plays into the hands of the political and military information managers.

The root of journalistic opposition to highly trained specialization is fiscal, not professional. It is simply cheaper to go on depending on general assignment reporters who supposedly can cover any story with equal competence, rather than investing in the training of specialists who will spend much of their time reading, traveling, and interviewing for stories that get into print or on the air only intermittently.

Whether or not this has been expressed in so many words, what the public has discerned, correctly, is that there is no place for the general assignment reporter in the coverage of major military operations, certainly not at any level above the division, air wing, or individual warship.[11]

So long as American journalism refuses to acknowledge that and to restructure itself accordingly, the government is duty-bound to restrict the activities of journalists in the severe manner imposed during the Persian Gulf War. Most certainly, it must not permit the use of equipment by which journalists can communicate directly by word or picture with editors and broadcast news executives outside the theater of operations. To permit the use of such technology by people at the level of understanding displayed during the televised press conferences would be tantamount to placing a loaded shotgun in the hands of a four-year-old.

There must also be a clear distinction between the access to U.S. military operations granted to competently trained American journalists and that accorded to foreign journalists. It is dangerous enough to grant access to an American who regards himself or herself as a "world journalist," free of such "middle class values" as patriotism. It is utterly impossible to determine the ultimate allegience of foreign reporters.

Do the restrictions on American journalists imposed during the Persian Gulf and certain to be imposed in the future if American journalism continues to resist change contain an element of danger for democratic government? Most certainly. To the degree that any aspect of government, in particular the military, is permitted to define how its activities are reported to the public there is a danger. But that danger must be weighted against the more immediate danger to the success of major military operations and to the personal safety of members of the armed forces.

It is the press itself, by adherence to outmoded concepts of organization and training, that has created the danger that now exists in the need for excessive military control, and it is only the press that can reduce those controls by beginning to act responsibly.

NOTES

1. William E. DePuy, "Keynote Address," *Armor* (July–August 1977): 34. In the same speech, fifteen years before his words would be confirmed in the deserts of Saudi Arabia and Iraq, DePuy said, "There is only one real Cavalry left in the Army and that is Air Cavalry. . . . The only real mobility differential we have is air mobility. . . . When the Germans broke open the World War I combat [pattern] in Poland in 1939 . . . they did it with Armor. We haven't broken open the armored warfare [pattern] of World War II. . . . The real question of the future is whether or not somebody will break the shell of that. . . . I think that someday there may be another breakthrough. . . . We have just got to keep our eye on that." (p. 34)

2. "The Keeper of Secrets in Chief," *New York Times*, 15 April 1986, p. B6.

3. Leslie Maitland Werner, "Meese Favors Reducing Total of Classified Data," *New York Times*, 21 March 1985, p. A25.

4. "State Secrecy Doesn't Help National Security" (Op Ed), *Wall Street Journal*, 18 June 1986.

5. "It Isn't Spying" (Editorial), *New York Times*, 4 March 1985.

6. U.S. Congress, House of Representatives, Committee on Government Operations, *Security Classification Policy and Executive Order 12356* (Washington, D.C.: U.S. Government Printing Office, 1982).

7. "The American press makes me think of a gigantic, super-modern fish cannery, a hundred floors high, capitalized at eleven billion dollars, and with tens of thousands of workers standing ready at the canning machines, but relying for its raw material on an inadequate number of handline fishermen in leaky rowboats." A. J. Liebling, "Goodbye M.B.I.," *The New Yorker*, 7 February 1948.

8. Novelist and sometime journalist and public official James H. Webb, Jr., "notes that some 330 newsmen covered the 1,200 Marines we once had in Lebanon, and that the two Marine companies on the perimeter were averaging 41 media visits each day." Paraphrased from the *San Diego Union* in *National Defense* 70 February 1986: 73.

9. Morley Safer, "Spying for Hanoi," *New York Times Magazine*, 11 March 1990, pp. 34–35, 87—92.

10. "Proposals in the 1840's and '50's to reform the [Chinese] civil service examinations in order to 'secure the services of capable men' in military affairs bore no fruit—at least partially because of the Board of Rites' insistence that scholars were men of breadth who 'need not be specialists.' " Richard J. Senith, "Educating Military Professionals 1875–1895" (Paper delivered at the annual meeting of the Association for Asian Studies, Chicago, 1978). So began China's century of humiliation.

11. "Aside from the Pentagon regulars . . . few members of the huge Washington press corps are familiar with defense issues. And yet the matters in which the Pentagon is involved are sometimes so important that the non-expert generalists . . . flow across the bridges . . . to handle the stories. They then disappear for weeks or months until the next crisis, which they greet with equal inexperience. This approach to covering Pentagon news cannot succeed. For several years as a reporter I tried it before finally moving to my own desk in the Pentagon press room . . . on a full-time basis. . . . Often while covering the Pentagon on a 20 percent basis, I fooled my editors and readers into thinking I was an expert . . . but I did not fool the official sources with whom I had to work. Members of the Washington press corps who attempt to dip in and out of the Pentagon on crisis stories or major issues cannot compete with a specialist in military affairs. The city editor in Chicago does not permit the reporter covering the business beat to handle a crisis story in City Hall, and the managing editor should not expect expert coverage of a military crisis or major defense story from a generalist . . . " Phil G. Goulding, *Confirm or Deny: Informing the People on National Security* (New York: Harper & Row, 1970), 219–20. Goulding is a former reporter for the *Cleveland Plain Dealer* and a former assistant secretary of defense for public affairs.

Epilogue

On May 21, 1992, fourteen months after the humiliating performance of the reporters covering the Persian Gulf War, Louis D. Boccardi, president of the AP, and other chief executives of print and broadcast news media obtained from the Department of Defense a nine-point "Statement of Principles" that will govern military-press relations in future emergencies.

"Open coverage" is the theme throughout, "except . . . "—the exceptions are huge:

- Except when pools "provide the only feasible means of early access to a military operation"
- Except "for specific events, such as those at extremely remote locations or where space is limited"
- Except when "Special Operations restrictions may limit access in some cases"

Any Pentagon staff officer who cannot use those "exceptions" to ensure tightly controlled, portal-to-portal pool operations should have his or her buttons snipped off.

Field commanders "will permit journalists to ride on military vehicles and aircraft whenever feasible." The Navy for its entire history has determined that "whenever feasible" means whenever there is assurance that the resulting prose and pictures will glorify the Navy and Marine Corps.

"Consistent with its capabilities" the press will be provided with facilities for the transmission of "pool material." When such facilities are unavailable, "journalists will, as always, file by any other means available," although "electromagnetic operational security . . . may require limited restrictions."

Any lawyer who advises a client to sign a contract like that should be disbarred.

In return for all of the concessions supposedly wrung from the military, "News organizations will make their best efforts to assign experienced journalists to combat operations and to make them familiar with U.S. military operations." How seriously the press regarded this part of the "Statement of Principles" can be judged from the fact that neither the *New York Times* nor the AP bothered to mention it when reporting the agreement.

In short, the military will control press coverage as it deems necessary or convenient by applying the exceptions and restrictions, and the press will make no serious effort to overcome that by changing its ways. The loser on all counts is, as usual, the public.

Select Bibliography

Adler, Ruth. *The Working Press: Special to the New York Times.* New York: Putnam's, 1966.

———. *A Day in the Life of the New York Times.* Philadelphia: Lippincott, 1971.

Agee, Warren Kendall. *The Press and Public Interest.* Washington, D.C.: Public Affairs, 1968.

Arlen, Michael. *The Living Room War.* New York: Viking, 1969.

Auletta, Ken. *Three Blind Mice: How the Networks Lost Their Way.* New York: Random House, 1991.

Bagdikian, Ben H. *The Information Machines: Their Impact on Men and the Media.* New York: Harper & Row, 1971.

———. *The Effete Conspiracy and Other Crimes by the Press.* New York: Harper & Row, 1972.

———. *The Media Monopoly.* Boston: Beacon, 1983.

Balk, Alfred. *A Free and Responsive Press.* New York: Twentieth Century Fund, 1973.

Barrett, Marvin, ed. *The Politics of Broadcasting.* New York: Crowell, 1973.

Barron, Jerome A. *Freedom of the Press for Whom? The Right of Access to Mass Media.* Bloomington: Indiana University, 1973.

Beech, Keyes. *Not Without the Americans, A Personal History.* New York: Doubleday, 1971.

Bray, Howard. *The Pillars of the Post: The Making of a News Empire in Washington.* New York: Norton, 1980.

Brown, Charles H. *The Correspondents' War.* New York: Scribners, 1967.

Cannon, Lou. *Reporting: An Inside View.* Sacramento, Calif.: Journal, 1977.

Cater, Douglas. *The Fourth Branch of Government.* New York: Random House, 1959.

———., ed. *Television as a Social Force: New Approaches to TV Criticism.* New York: Praeger, 1975.

Catledge, Turner. *My Life and Times*. New York: Harper & Row, 1971.

Davison, Walter P., ed. *Mass Communications Research: Major Issues and Future Directions*. New York: Praeger, 1974.

Diamond, Edward. *The Tin Kazoo*. Boston: MIT, 1975.

Emery, Edwin. *The Press and America: An Interpretative History of the Mass Media*. Englewood Cliffs, N.J.: Prentice-Hall, 1972.

Epstein, Edward J. *Between Fact and Fiction: The Problem of Journalism*. New York: Vintage, 1975.

———. *The Televised War: In Between Fact and Fiction*. New York: Vintage, 1975.

Fang, Irving. *Television News*. New York: Hastings, 1972.

Fehrenbach, T. R. *This Kind of War*. New York: Macmillan, 1963.

Fialka, John J. *Hotel Warriors: Covering the Gulf War*. Washington, D.C.: Woodrow Wilson Center, 1992.

Flood, Charles B. *War of the Innocents*. New York: McGraw-Hill, 1970.

Frank, Reuven. *The Brief Wonderful Life of Network News*. New York: Simon & Schuster, 1991.

Fulbright, J. W. *The Pentagon Propaganda Machine*. New York: Liveright, 1970.

Gans, Herbert J. *Deciding What's News: A Study of 'CBS Evening News,' 'NBC Nightly News,' 'Newsweek,' and 'Time.'* New York: Pantheon, 1979.

Graham, Fred P. *Press Freedoms Under Pressure*. New York: Twentieth Century Fund, 1972.

Griffith, Thomas. *How True: A Skeptic's Guide to Believing the News*. Boston: Atlantic–Little, Brown, 1976.

Halperin, Morton H., and Hoffman, Daniel N. *Top Secret: National Security and the Right to Know*. Washington, D.C.: New Republic, 1977.

Harris, Robert. *Gotcha! The Media, the Government and the Falklands Crisis*. London: Faber & Faber, 1983.

Heise, Juergen Arthur. *Minimum Disclosure: How the Pentagon Manipulates the News*. New York: Norton, 1979.

Higgins, Marguerite. *The Report of a Woman Combat Correspondent*. New York: Doubleday, 1951.

Hohenberg, John. *The News Media: A Journalist Looks at His Profession*. New York: Holt, Rinehart & Winston, 1968.

———. *Free Press, Free People: The Best Cause*. New York: Columbia University, 1971.

Hooper, Alan. *The Military and the Media*. Brookfield, Vt.: Gower, 1982.

Krieghbaum, Hillier. *Pressures on the Press*. New York: Crowell, 1972.

Lichter, S. Robert; Lichter, Sandra S.; and Rothman, Stanley. *The Media Elite*. New York: Adler & Adler, 1986.

MacArthur, John R. *Censorship and Propaganda in the Gulf War*. New York: Hill & Wang, 1992.

MacNeil, Robert. *The People Machine*. New York: Harper & Row, 1968.

Marshall, S.L.A. *Bringing Up the Rear*. San Francisco, Calif.: Presidio, 1980.

Matthews, Joseph J. *Reporting the Wars*. Minneapolis: University of Minnesota, 1957.

Mecklin, John. *Mission in Torment*. New York: Doubleday, 1965.

Merrill, John C. *The Elite Press: Great Newspapers of the World*. New York: Pitman, 1968.

Mitchell, Burroughs. *The Education of an Editor*. New York: Doubleday, 1980.

Mock, James Robert. *Censorship 1917*. Princeton, N.J.: Princeton University, 1941.

Mott, Franklin L. *American Journalism: A History: 1690–1960*. New York: Macmillan, 1960.

Oberdorfer, Don. *Tet*. New York: Doubleday, 1971.

Powers, Ron. *The Newscasters*. New York: St. Martin's, 1977.

Quinn, Sally. *We're Going to Make You a Star*. New York: Simon & Schuster, 1975.

Rather, Dan (with Mickey Herskowitz). *The Camera Never Blinks*. New York: Morrow, 1977.

Ratscha, Robert M. *Foreign Affairs News and the Broadcast Journalist*. New York: Praeger, 1975.

Reston, James B. *The Artillery of the Press: Its Influence on American Foreign Policy*. New York: Harper & Row, 1967.

Rivers, William L. *Responsibility in Mass Communication*. New York: Harper & Row, 1968.

———. *The Adversaries*. Boston: Beacon, 1970.

———. *The Mass Media and Modern Society*. New York: Holt, Rinehart & Winston, 1971.

Roshco, Bernard. *Newsmaking*. Chicago, Illinois: University of Chicago, 1979.

Salisbury, Harrison. *Without Fear or Favor: The New York Times and Its Times*. New York: Times Books, 1980.

Schorr, Daniel. *Clearing the Air*. New York: Houghton Mifflin, 1977.

Schramm, Wilbur Lang, and Roberts, Donald F., eds. *The Process and Effects of Mass Communication*. Urbana: University of Illinois, 1971.

Sheehan, Neil. *A Bright Shining Lie*. New York: Random House, 1988.

Small, William. *To Kill a Messenger: Television News and the Real World*. New York: Hastings, 1970.

Smith, Perry. *How CNN Fought the Gulf War: View from the Inside*. Secaucus, N.J.: Carroll Publishing Group, 1992.

Sobel, Robert. *The Manipulators: America in the Media Age*. New York: Anchor, 1976.

Stein, Robert. *Media Power: Who Is Shaping Your Picture of the World?* Boston: Houghton Mifflin, 1972.

Steinberg, Charles Side. *The Communications Arts: An Introduction to Mass Media*. New York: Hastings, 1970.

Talese, Gay. *The Kingdom and the Power*. New York: World, 1969.

Thompson, Loren B., ed. *Defense Beat: The Dilemmas of Defense Coverage*. New York: Lexington, 1991.

Turner, Kathleen J. *Lyndon Johnson's Dual War: Vietnam and the Press*. Chicago, Illinois: University of Chicago, 1985.

Voelker, Francis, ed. *Mass Media Forces in Our Society*. New York: Harcourt Brace Jovanovich, 1972.

Weiner, Robert. *Live from Baghdad: Gathering News at Ground Zero*. New York: Doubleday, 1992.

Wiggins, James Russell. *Freedom or Secrecy*. New York: Oxford, 1965.

Index

About the Author

WILLIAM V. KENNEDY began a career as a professional journalist as a 17-year-old cub reporter in 1945, and a military career as an enlisted man in the Regular Army in 1946. He has pursued both of these careers since. His work as a journalist specializing in military affairs has been published in all principal U.S. military journals and many U.S. and foreign professional and commercial journals and newspapers, including all major U.S. daily newspapers. He has served on active duty as an Intelligence Officer in the Strategic Air Command and as an Army Public Affairs Officer in the Pentagon, retiring from the Army Reserve in 1982 as a Colonel. From 1967 to 1984 he served as a civilian member of the U.S. Army War College Strategic Studies Institute and U.S. Army War College Faculty, returning to full-time military journalism in 1984. He is a principal author of *The Intelligence War* (1983), an internationally recognized text on the subject.